KLEE

by
Constance Naubert-Riser

Introduction by
Gualtieri di San Lazzaro

Translated by John Greaves

PORTLAND HOUSE
NEW YORK

Originally published by Fernand Hazan, Paris 1988

This edition published 1988 by Portland House
Distributed by Crown Publishers, Inc.
225 Park Avenue South
New York, New York 10003

Reprinted 1990

ISBN 0-517-64792-3

Printed and bound in Hong Kong

h g f e d c b

FROM BERN TO MUNICH
THE APPRENTICESHIP YEARS

Paul Klee was born on 18th December 1879 in the schoolhouse at Munchenbuchsee near Bern. His father had once been a professional singer, but was now a music teacher. Shortly after Klee's birth, the family moved into the city of Bern itself. Klee inherited his father's caustic temperament, but the rough edges were smoothed by the serenity of his mother, Ida Maria, and were apparent in the young Paul's fine sense of humour. He also inherited his parents' musical aptitudes. He played the violin very well and was, at one stage, considering the serious pursuit of voice studies, much to the delight of his family. Ida Maria and Hans Klee also had a daughter, Mathilde; we know her from her brother's portrait. It seems she had little influence on Paul, but her life-long devotion to her brother was absolute.

At a time when so many artists were irremediably drawn to rebellion by the incomprehension of, and hostility towards, their medium, Paul's pursuit of his vocation was obstacle free; he enjoyed the approval and encouragement of his parents. The originality and boldness in Klee's work came simply as an extension of his own personality.

Hans Klee was more than a father; he was also a good friend. In an exchange of moving letters with Klee the elder, the young fine arts student first confessed his early artistic ambitions and the enthusiasm inspired in him by masterpieces hanging in the Munich Pinakothek. Klee senior was an indulgent, if ironic, character and, according to Marguerite Frey Surbeck, a man whose lucidity of judgement was unrelenting. He was young Klee's first real ally, the first supporter of the artist's work.

Paul drew and painted with his left hand. He wasn't completely left-handed; he wrote with his right. His son Felix tells us that he could, in fact, draw and paint equally well with both hands simultaneously. To a certain extent this explains the tremendous liberty, the self-intoxicated fantasy of line to which Klee's graphicism owes much of its charm. At school, his notebooks were covered in drawings. He drew ceaselessly, one ear on the class in progress. Only Greek lessons seemed to touch his poetic nature and hold his attention.

Soon after he left school, Klee put an advertisement in the student magazine to which he had enthusiastically contributed. This notice offered, in abundant quantities, 'Madonnas, reformed Magdalenes, young girls and ruffians selected from the notebooks of a sixth-form student'.

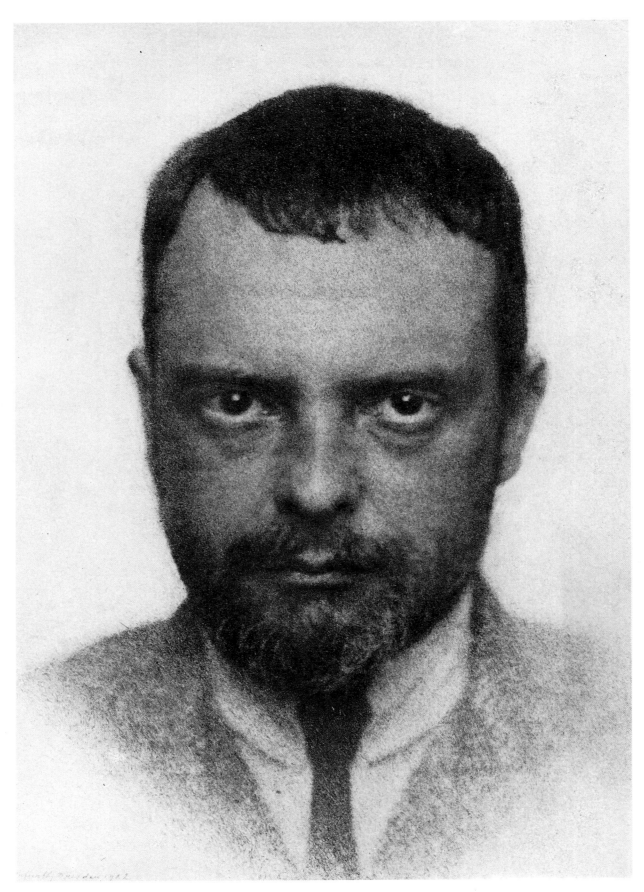

Klee in 1922 (photo Hugo Erfurth)

Like most boys of his age, young Klee was obsessed by the problem of sex. In his *Diaries* he tells us that he was precociously seduced by the beauty of little girls at the tender age of 3, and that he even wanted to become a little girl himself so that he could wear lace-trimmed knickers. His first loves (he was 7 at the time) were a schoolgirl from Bern and a young lady from France (or perhaps a French-speaking Swiss). He speaks also of a certain Camille to whom he remained faithful for all of five years; later a cousin from Basel attracted his amorous attentions. However, these affairs were to prove of little consequence. Having passed his examinations, he decided to commit himself seriously to painting and, at the age of 19, set off for Munich.

As evidence of the three years spent in Munich studying painting, first in Professor Knirr's private school, then at the Academy under Stuck, we have only the artist's account and a few relatively insignificant works. Klee consoled himself with the courtship of a young pianist, Lily Stumpf, who managed to persuade her parents to invite him home one Christmas Eve. Although he pursued his amorous inclinations elsewhere, he was falling more and more for Lily, whose taste in music he shared. Lily declared herself ready to wait as long as necessary, be it an age; the essential thing was not to compromise her fiancé's artistic career.

At the Academy, he was becoming more sure of himself. Stuck, not given to over-encouragement, occasionally found Klee's illustrations 'original' and suggested that he should present them to the review *Jugend*.

Having spent the summer of 1901 with his family in Bern, Klee was preparing for a trip to Italy with his friend Hermann Haller, whom he had known since 1886.

In October 1901 Paul, with Haller, who would one day become a well-known sculptor, crossed the border into Italy. In Milan he admired Tintoretto in La Brera, but it was Genoa that really opened his eyes to Italy. It was the first port he had ever seen and gave him his first ever vision of the sea, spreading before him like pictures in an exhibition. From Genoa they went on to Livorno which rather bored him. If Genoa was a 'dramatic 'city, Rome captivated him with its 'epic' magic. A few months later the magic had worn thin and his preference switched to Naples whose aquarium would, many years later, inspire some of his most sumptuous compositions. Certain lights, a glaucous tone here, a translucent depth there, a delicate iridescence, consistently run through Klee's work and are an indelible testament to these early emotional experiences.

In 1902, after an absence of seven months, he returned to Bern a changed man. Despite the Pan-like beard, grown in deference to the statues of antiquity, the new Klee was no Pan amongst the reeds. Here was a man who wanted to reach the top of the ladder and stay there. From now on he had but one goal: to conquer life.

Between 1902 and 1906 he made remarkable technical progress, which he recorded in his *Diaries*. His etchings and, later, the *sous-verres* allowed him to take on the problem of line; the line with which he would one day succeed in giving full vent to his poetic imagination. This is the line which, like Ariadne's thread, would lead him out of the labyrinth of difficult times. We must agree with him when he says that he discovered his style in the process of his initiation into the techniques of engraving on zinc or glass. The expressionism in these engravings – *The Virgin in a Tree, Comedian, The Monarchist, Woman and Beast, The Threatening Head* – is, none the less, caricatural; whereas the *sous-verres*, glass plates covered with tar and colours engraved with a needle, were a preparation for the alchemy of the great years, for the fulsome grace of his tonal effect. Sometimes he would complain that his work process was stymied, only to announce some days later that he had succeeded in bending nature to his stylistic design.

Because of military service, he was obliged to take various medical examinations in Munich which resulted in his classification as a reserve recruit. He took advantage of these moments to spend time with Lily and 'to kiss youthfulness on the mouth before it took flight'. He also went to Berlin where the critic Heilbut tried in vain to put on an exhibition of Klee's prints and to publish some reproductions in the review *Kunst und Künstler*. Several people visited Klee in Bern, especially Lily. Their love was now beyond question, and it is certain that without her he would have had less confidence in himself. Lily's father, however, was less enthusiastic about the romance and the couple were forced to meet in secret.

Music, literature and new relationships enriched the artist's existence. If, sometimes, he appeared to accept advice without question, as soon as he recognized a divergence of direction he would not hesitate to part company, regardless of the support he might previously have enjoyed.

In May 1905, in the company of his friends Moilliet and Bloesch, he set off to realize one of his most cherished dreams: a two-week trip to Paris. This first contact with the City of Light, however, was less than decisive. Paul was not yet mature enough to take on modern art with the assurance he had shown *vis-à-vis* the ancients in Italy. He was suspicious of this new domain. He visited the Louvre and the Luxembourg Museum; he wandered through the principal *quartiers*; he admired the civic monuments. In the evenings he frequented the theatres, the dance-halls and the cafés. The Comédie Française, the Opera, the Opera Comique, the Bal Bullier and the Taverne de l'Olympia all appear in his *Diaries*. Above all else, he was delighted to discover Da Vinci; but he also admired Tintoretto and Watteau, whom he considered

Paul Klee and Hermann Haller in Rome, 1901

great painters; Goya, whose sonorities he found ravishing; Millet, whose *Printemps* was 'magnificent'; and, finally, Rembrandt, particularly the later period. He also noted Poussin, Claude Lorrain, Ingres, Courbet, Corot, Franz Hals and Chardin, whom he found 'monumental in the small format'. He liked the moderns less. Puvis de Chavannes he saw as inspiration for the early Holder. In Manet he discerned the influence of Goya and Velasquez, but considered that he knew how to transform these influences, 'gradually coming over to the present'. Monet's painting seemed uneven to him, rich but over-impulsive; Sisley's work was 'refined'; Pissaro's 'more tart'. Carrière, whose preoccupations came close to Klee's own, seemed a good model for tonality. Although he admired Renoir, he thought he was lightweight, bordering on bad taste.

Meanwhile, Klee had finished his anatomical studies in Bern with Professor Strasser. He no longer found work tiresome, as he used to do in Munich, and the notion that what he was learning would some day be of use encouraged him to persevere. He was reading a lot of Oscar

Wilde, from whom he learned that art was 'appearance and symbol'. He copied out certain passages from *De Profundis* (on *Hamlet*) and long quotes from other books. Reading for Klee was an endless means of correcting himself through the control of his reactions. 'Even yesterday I might have rejected *The Portrait of Dorian Gray*; today I enjoyed it; two days ago it probably would have intoxicated me.' So struck was he by *Candide* that he was later driven to illustrate it. He was an assiduous concertgoer. He heard Pablo Casals, whom he considered to be one of the greatest musicians of all time. These two passions, music and literature, underline the Germanic side of Klee's personality.

The more his inclinations towards art were confirmed, the stronger became his need to live in a big city. 'Even for Lily's sake, it would be good to get away from the family home. We would work together, I don't know for how long.'

At last, in September 1906, Lily's father's resistance worn down; Klee officially announced his engagement. The wedding was held in Bern some weeks later and the couple moved directly to Munich, living first in a little boarding-house in Furstenstrasse, then in a small flat in Ainmillerstrasse. Lily gave piano lessons and Paul, who had hankered so long for an end to his solitude, wrote in his *Diaries*: 'In this town of five thousand painters, I'm quite alone.'

The first years in Munich, from 1906 to 1912, were years of learning and fruitful encounters. He went to see the impressionists in Basel in 1906 and again in a Munich gallery in 1907. In the same year, still in Munich, he saw one Toulouse-Lautrec collection and two Van Gogh exhibitions. His Swiss friend Ernst Sonderegger introduced him to Daumier and Ensor etchings. Klee speaks of Cézanne for the first time in 1909 after admiring eight of the French painter's pictures at the Sezession. 'In my eyes

Mathilde, Lily and Paul Klee in Bern, 1906

he is the teacher *par excellence*, much more of a teacher than Van Gogh.'

In 1911 he finally met Kandinsky, the event coinciding with what could be considered the end of the Bern apprenticeship period – the period of impetuousness and excessive enthusiasm which had been necessary to reassure both himself and Lily. When, to pay his way, Klee presented his drawings to *Simplizissimus* (1906), he nevertheless refused to go along with the paper's editorial direction. Then, as always, in his desire 'to conquer life', he depended solely on a policy of eschewing all compromise, and for this reason he temporarily took up modest employment in a local night-school.

Klee was no longer isolated. A small circle of friends surrounded and supported him: his childhood friends Bloesch and the Swiss painters Kreydolf and Welti. The painter Thomann from Zurich asked him to join the Walze Society. Thanks to Louis Moilliet, he met Auguste Macke in the summer of 1911, at Gunten, on the banks of Lake Thun. Macke knew Kandinsky, who was now living in Munich, a stone's throw from Klee's house. 'Onkel

The Schubert Quintet in Munich, 1900
  (Paul Klee on the right)

Luli' (Louis Moilliet) visited Kandinsky whenever he was in Munich. He showed him Klee's work and brought back some of Kandinsky's non-figurative pieces to show the younger artist. After their meeting in the autumn, other new friends also encouraged him: Franz Marc, who was to be the closest, Campendonk, Jawlensky, Marianne von Werefkin and Gabriele Munter, the amazon of abstract art. All supporters of Klee, they formed a group which became known later that year to the Munich public as *Der Blaue Reiter*.

Kandinsky was to have a profound influence on his young friend, especially as Klee was now mature enough for this decisive encounter. In 1910 he had written 'it is more important to know how to concentrate on your paint-box than to study nature. I must one day be able to play freely on the keyboard of my colours.' Furthermore, his exploration of light had admirably prepared him for an equally significant meeting, some months later in Paris, with Robert Delaunay, in April 1912. Klee found Kandinsky's work 'sehr merkwurdig' – strange and remarkable. 'Kandinsky', he wrote in his *Diaries*, 'has an exceptionally good head, fine and clear'. His admiration for the Russian was growing and growing. In an article for a Swiss review, he wrote about the first *Blaue Reiter* exhibition at the Thannhauser in these terms: 'the most daring of all is Kandinsky; he tries to convince you, even with words'.

Klee was invited to participate in the second *Blaue Reiter* exhibition, featuring just drawings and etchings. At this time, Klee was not yet aware of the influence Kandinsky was having on him, through his painting, his theories and, above all, his book *The Spiritual in Art*. Admiring though he was, he preferred Franz Marc, perhaps simply because Kandinsky was much older and intimidated him. Nevertheless, it was with Kandinsky that he would share, spiritually speaking, a large section of the road ahead.

THE '*BLAUE REITER*' PERIOD

Klee's second trip to Paris would not have had the importance rightly attributed to it by critics if the painter had not given over three hours, in these memorable two weeks, to Robert Delaunay. These were three hours during which his doubts dissolved and, artistically speaking, he gained years.

He deposited his young son Felix with his grandparents in Bern and left for Paris, arriving on 2nd April 1912. His wife, coming from Munich, arrived a few hours earlier. Paul and Lily wanted to do everything at once. Like all tourists, they strolled along the boulevards and along the Seine, visited Notre-Dame, the Latin Quarter, Sainte-Chapelle . . . Apart from one night at the Opera, where they saw a performance of *Rigoletto*, and another evening at the Ballet, they spent their time at the popular cabarets at the Tabarin, the Moulin de la Galette, the Bal Bullier and the Gaietée Montparnasse. Needless to say, they also took in the Louvre, the Luxembourg Museum and the Salon des Indépendants.

On 11th April, Klee went to see Delaunay at his *atelier* in the rue des Grands Augustins opposite a now-derelict convent. Sonia Delaunay was to remember little or nothing of this visit; a young man came to see her husband, that was all. Klee was unknown. About this meeting, which was to have such an influence on his career, Klee, in his *Diaries*, writes only: [1912] 'In the morning I visited Delaunay in his studio.' He says nothing about the paintings Delaunay certainly showed him, or about their conversation – perhaps the reason is that his days were so full that he had no time to concentrate on himself. Lily didn't leave him alone for a moment and they got home late every night. The very day of the Delaunay visit, Lily wanted to go to the Bal Bullier because Paul had told her so much about it.

Robert Delaunay was second husband to Sonia, a young and beautiful artist and a fine painter in her own right. The day after this memorable encounter, Paul, with his wife and his friends Haller and Sonderegger, went to see the German art critic and dealer, Wilhelm Uhde, Sonia's first husband, whose collection had already been shown in Munich. In Paris, Uhde was looking for works by Henri Rousseau, Picasso and Braque with a view to assembling an exclusive collection of 'naïve' painting. Another expatriate German in Paris was Daniel-Henry Kahnweiler. Just before going back to Bern, Klee paid him a visit and saw some more cubist canvasses, along with others by Derain and De Vlaminck. He also met Le Fauconnier, a painter who enjoyed not inconsiderable esteem at this time. On 16th April they went to see the impressionist dealer, Durand-Ruel, who, in the manner of the Roman emperors, admitted an audience, but only once a week. On the same day, in the Bernheim-Jeune gallery, they stood in admiration before Matisse and Goya. The next day, exhausted but content, Lily returned to Munich. The night before she had witnessed the signing of a hundred lithographic plates by Klee. His *Diaries* shed little light on this event. He simply notes: 'Evening, signed a hundred lithographs', and doesn't indicate which works were in question. Paul went back to Bern to pick up Felix and returned home. The young artist's stay in Paris had been salutary and extremely profitable.

Later in 1912, speaking of Robert Delaunay, he said, in a celebrated comment which revealed the high regard in which he held the author of *Fenêtres*, 'One of the most intelligent artists of our times, and the one who suffered most from this inconsistency'. He contrasts him with the cubists he had discovered in Paris. 'In the field of landscapes, cubism has already learned how to win over the public, but it seems to me, in terms of form, they are not able to avoid the ridiculous. I bring this up, firstly because certain inconsistencies in cubism I find uncomfortable, but above all, to insist on what justifies the ultimate step: knowing how to omit the object.'

In sum, Klee reproached the cubists for their 'destruction for the love of construction'. Delauney remedied this, he adds, 'in an astonishingly simple manner, creating the kind of painting which is self-sufficient, borrowing nothing from nature but, which, from the point of view of form, has an entirely abstract existence. Moreover, and let's be sure about this, we are talking about a living plastic creation, as far removed from a tapestry as is a Bach fugue.'

This text is critical. It illuminates both Klee's thinking and his temperament, while setting down, in its lucid criticism of cubism. the principle of autonomous art which was to find its expression in Klee himself; a principle to which all future non-figurative painters would be obliged to refer.

What Klee particularly admired in Delaunay, and would appreciate later in the Italian futurists, is movement. What he condemned in cubism was its immobility. Elsewhere in his *Diaries* we read: 'Ingres is said to have ordered the motionless, I want to go beyond pathos and order motion.' And how eagerly he took to the task of translating the article Delaunay sent him for *Der Sturm*, one of the first modern art reviews in Europe.

Delaunay wrote: 'Impressionism is the birth of light in painting. Light reaches us through sensibility; without visual sensibility, no light, no movement. Light creates the movement of colours in nature. Movement is created by the relationship between the uneven proportions of colours contrasting between themselves; and this is what constitutes *reality*. This reality has the property of *depth* (we can see as far as the stars), and therefore becomes *rhythmic simultaneity*. Simultaneity in light is *harmony*, the *rhythm of colours* which forms *the vision of man*. Human

Klee, *Young Man Resting,* 1911

vision is endowed with the greatest reality of all since it comes to us directly from contemplation of the universe. Vision is our most elevated sense; the sense which most directly communicates *consciousness* to the brain, the idea of the world's vital movement; its movement is *simultaneity*.'

These ideas expressed in a language which vigorously attacked all conformist theory and syntax – were familiar to Klee. In 1910 he noted in his *Diaries*: 'Producing light by illuminating tones is ancient history. Light conceived as a movement of colours is already a much newer idea.' All in all, Delaunay and Klee spoke the same language and shared the same preoccupations. The French painter was already well known in Germany. Five of his paintings featured in the first *Blaue Reiter* exhibition (December 1911–January 1912). In his *Saint-Severin* he boldly confronted the problem of space and perspective, which had a considerable influence on the young de Chirico, who, like Klee, studied painting in Munich. Klee was drawn as much to naturalism as to abstraction, and could as little tear himself away from the one as he could completely commit himself to the other. In Delaunay, neo-impressionism's heir apparent, he found a guide and an example to follow, whereas Kandinsky, while taking his colours from nature, from his side pushed Klee towards abstraction.

In 1913, Klee made another important acquaintance: the young Arp, who, at the age of 25, had already organized an avant-garde exhibition in Zurich. Klee gave the young unknown a warm welcome. He showed him several drawings, notably the twenty-six *Candide* illustrations, and also the graphic commentaries composed to accompany certain Morgenstern poems.

Contrary to critical opinion, which considered the *Astonishing Beasts* of 1912 puerile, the Klee of 1925, characteristically capricious and brusque, was already

present, even in a context of geometric schema. Rather less significant are the drawings which followed, like the naïvely caricatural *Fleeing Policemen*. Arp, particularly struck by the *Candide* illustrations, promised to present them to his friend Otto Flake, another Alsacian, who enjoyed a certain prestige with the publishers Weissen Bücher.

Some time later, Klee visited an exhibition of Arp and his friends on which he wrote an article for a review. Then he went to see Arp at his home near Weggis. The Arps lived an isolated existence. The father had left Alsace after the war of 1870–1 to set up a small factory business

Klee, *He Lifts the Veil with a Timid Hand*, illustration for *Candide* by Voltaire, ch. 7, 1911–1912

in Switzerland. Arp received Paul Klee with full honours, befitting the arrival of a great man.

Arp always mantained that it was he who persuaded Weissen Bücher to publish the German translation of *Candide* with Klee's illustrations. But Klee's biography informs us that nothing came of his efforts until 1920 when *Candide* did appear, published by Kurt Wolff in Munich.

Unlike cubism, Italian futurism, which advocated movement, immediately appealed to Klee. He declared that Carrà was a 'great talent' who makes one think of Tintoretto or Delacroix, 'so related are the sonorities of his colour and even the spirit of his execution'. Boccioni and Severini, he adds, are a good deal further from the old masters, but he considers them 'very good none the less'. Despite these admittedly *risqué* assessements, the influence of cubism on Klee is more evident than that of the futurists. With Klee, the first judgement is rarely the most pertinent. Of course, he was not completely wrong in thinking of Tintoretto and Delacroix; but what he must

Klee, *He Pierces it Right Through*, illustration for *Candide* by Voltaire, ch. 9, 1911–1912

really have appreciated in futurism were Boccioni's theories on the 'state of the soul', against which he could measure his own.

1913 was a very important year. Things looked promising for Klee. The publisher, Piper, planned a portfolio dedicated to the expressionists and wanted Klee to be represented; and Walden, the publisher of *Sturm*, suggested an exhibition alongside Franz Marc and Kubin, which turned out to be the famous Autumn Salon in Berlin, to which Klee contributed twenty-two works. But an even more significant event was to take place: the trip to Tunisia, which would completely eclipse these early successes, however long overdue.

THE SOUTHERN MOON

After fifteen years of study, experiments, doubts, certainties and fertile encounters, the name of Paul Klee was still known only to a small circle of friends and admirers. Despite a few dazzling revelations, Klee was not yet the poet and painter we admire today.

In April 1914, a voyage to Tunisia was decided and embarked upon. The initiative came from his friend Louis Moilliet (who was later to have a painting accepted by the Basel Museum in 1916 – the first work of modern art to hang in a Swiss gallery). Moilliet knew a Swiss doctor in Tunis by the name of Jäggi who had once invited him to Tunisia. This time Moilliet proposed that his friends Klee and Macke should accompany him. A pharmacist from Bern provided the funds necessary for the expedition by buying some paintings.

On Sunday 5th April the three friends arrived in Marseilles. Paul was infatuated with the place and would have quite happily stayed. The Germans marvelled at the poetry of the old docks and were immediately taken by the opposition between the tranquillity of the old Mediterranean city and the animated bustle of the port. Klee could not help but be seduced.

On 6th April the painters went aboard the *Carthage*, a new steamer of the Transatlantic Company. During the voyage Klee let himself be swept away by the magical colours 'of the air and the water', anticipating the great revelation to come at Kairouan.

'My father', said Paul Klee later, 'was always pro-

Gabriele Münter, *Man in an Armchair*, 1913

foundly sensitive to the call of the South.' In Tunis, at Dr Jäggi's country house, in Carthage and at Kairouan, Klee seemed to be rediscovering personal memories. 'Could this be my homeland?' he asked himself in Kairouan. Without losing his sense of humour ('a bit monotonous this Arab music', he admitted in his *Diaries*, 'but the belly-dancing is interesting; we don't see anything like that at home') he had the feeling of coming back to the civilization to which he owed his deep Spanish or Moorish eyes. For a while, he forgot his fine theories of line and simultaneous contrasts of colour. He painted water-colours in which form is virtually a matter of accident. If he happened to be thinking of any particular masters as models during these days, we can only guess who they were. It is certain, though, that he had not forgotten Cézanne; his water-colours confirm that. His tone-washes are less dense; his brush-strokes are broader. The division of space into vertical or horizontal bands recalls Delaunay.

The pages given over to these unforgettable two weeks in Klee's *Diaries* radiate well-being, physical well-being above all, a kind of calm confidence in his own possibilities. It is with an assured eye that he surveys the long road ahead. There are no longer the unreasoned outbursts, the stabs and the jerks, but rather, a deeply reasoned certitude. Klee's lyricism, which from now on nothing was to quell, was born one Easter Sunday on the southern Mediterranean coast at St-Germain, near Tunis. The evening before, for the benefit of his host's children, the painter had decorated and hidden Easter eggs in the garden. Some days previously he had witnessed a burial on the outskirts of the town. Six mules had dragged the funeral carriage with its coffin, all gold and azure-blue. Around the hearse, women had engaged in a noisy lament. On this balmy Easter evening, the accumulation of impressions – the melancholy landscape, the tearful palm trees, the colours

of the air and the sea, the denser sonority of the port, the starry sky, the immense new moon, the crushing midday heat, the encounter with the blue-and-gold funeral carriage, the eggs hidden in the greenery – were all revived in Klee like a fairy story. 'Distant still, very distant, but very precise nonetheless.' It was a tale of a thousand and one nights that Paul would retell over and over again. 'The evening is deep inside me forever. Many a blond, northern moonrise, like a muted reflection, will softly remind me, and remind me again and again. It will be my bride, my *alter ego*. An incentive to find myself. I myself am the moonrise of the South.'

Klee discovered, then, in the very depths of his being, the treasure of real poetry. It was like something that had lain hidden, withdrawn into itself, and all of a sudden had blossomed out, freeing his imagination which, from now on, even when cautious or constrained, would be forever effervescent and alive. His atavistic contradictions were finally resolved. Some days later at Kairouan he would say: 'Colour is in me. I don't have to search to grasp it. I know it will possess me forever, I know it. That is the meaning of this wonderful moment: Colour and I will always be as one. I am a painter.' Thus, as the poet awakened, so did the painter. But in Klee's life as in his work, it is the poetic emotion which precedes the plastic expression.

The water-colours he took back to Bern: *View of Saint-Germain, Hamammet Motif* and *In Front of the Gates of Kairouan*, are minor works compared with the images he had stored within him – the moon, the full southern moon, the disquieting crescent of Islam, the Bible star, the strange plants, the little domes, the greenness, the orange trees, the saffron yellow of the sand and the ochre of the scorched earth, the whiteness of the architecture, the tents, the banderoles, mysterious signs like truncated Arabic characters, the graphic weave of some of his compositions – so many resonances, the memory of which nothing could ever erase. The little square Arabian houses inspired in him a rather unorthodox cubism. And was he perhaps asking to be forgiven for taking liberties when he painted his extraordinary *Homage to Picasso*, a combination of brown and grey rectangles and squares, framed in an oval?

Unlike other occidentals discovering the Orient, Klee did not indulge in orgies of the paint-box. One should not expect from him artificial raptures and gushing colour but, rather, a perfect consonance of tonalities or the unique, vibrating note of a single spot concentrating in itself all the lustre of a precious stone. Klee rarely gives us a symphony. Contemplating this work or that, we are more likely to sense the bright laughter of a brook or the trilling of a bird in the silence of the woods. Seeing is not enough, we must listen to the painting. He is, above all, a painter of 'sensation'. As Bonnard once said: 'he produces an hermetic world, the painting is like a book which carries its interest from place to place. One can imagine this artist spending a lot of his time looking around and within himself.'

In the last years of his life, Klee was to rediscover Islam and the works of his late period will bear the trace of the long dream which had been fostered in him during the trip to Tunisia.

In Tunis, on the eve of departure, Klee experienced a sudden need to be alone, to eat 'solemnly alone' in the best Italian restaurant. And alone he embarked for Palermo, in the third class. In Naples and then in Rome he felt as if he had returned after only a few days' absence. In fact, twelve years had gone by since his first trip to Italy. He didn't stop at Florence. In Milan he only waited long enough to take the next train to Bern. Had he run out of funds, or was his haste due to a fear of dissipating *en route* his treasure-trove of images and sensations that he wanted to take home intact? In any event, without this treasure, stored and protected in his heart, the impending war, the very idea of which was an affront to his reason, would have been too cruel for him to bear, perhaps even fatal. The trip to Tunisia, with its incalculable impact on Paul Klee, had taken less than three weeks.

EVERYTHING BECAME KLEE

It was during the war that 'everything became Klee'. Shortly after his return from Tunisia, and after the start of hostilities about which Klee had had a foreboding of gratuitous horror (to be manifested in certain drawings from the *Book of Images of 'Sturm'*, published in 1918, although some go back as far as 1913), he succeeded in uniting painting, and poetry, particularly in the ideograms which he called 'script-pictures'. But are not all his works, in a certain sense, script-pictures?

The war turned Paul Klee away from the troubled world and forced him to retreat within himself for sanctuary. In a happy world it is good to look around oneself; in a world which is materially and morally in ruins, consolation can only be found in the memory of exquisite, intensely-lived moments.

Two movements were born in this period: Dada in Zurich and metaphysical painting in Italy. The first was essentially negating; the second was ambitious and reflective. In Klee the two tendencies are balanced. He is Dada even in his most serious and meditative works: everything becomes Klee, but as in a dream, a kind of waking dream. Also, we should not forget that the surrealists recognized Klee as one of their most important precursors. Klee, taking his inspiration from the new tendencies, from Delaunay and the cubist experiments, rethought as a poet the plastic elements of the painting: movement, space and light.

It is hardly surprising that such a sensitive being should have sought retreat from the anguish of his time in total self-absorption in his work. 'I have carried this war inside me for a long time', he wrote. 'And that is why, internally, it no longer concerns me'. All his friends were in uniform or far away, like Kandinsky, who had returned to Russia, and Jawlensky, back with Frau von Werefkin in Switzerland. Weissen Bücher were hesitant about publishing *Candide* because, like most publishers, they were reluctant to take decisions, preferring to shut themselves away in hostile silence. A single ray of light on a bleak horizon was an association, beginning in 1915, with Rilke, who was already famous as the author of *Book of Hours* and *Notebooks of Malte Laurids Brigge*.

Rilke and Klee saw a lot of each other, sometimes in the painter's little apartment, sometimes in the spacious studio which Rilke shared with his friend, the blonde Lou Albert-Lasard, herself a painter. To keep discussion of war to a minimum at these meetings, Klee organized concerts, with the participation of his wife and a few musician friends. One day, the painter was good enough to bring Rilke sixty of his colour compositions for him to contemplate at his leisure over a period of months. Thus it was that the poet gained an acute understanding of the transition from naturalism to abstraction in art, and, more specifically, in Klee's painting. He discussed this subject in a letter to his friend Baladine on 28th February 1921. It is useful to recall that Baladine Klossowska, a painter herself and mother of the painter Bonnard, was to play an important rôle in Rilke's life between 1919 and 1926. He called her Merline. Rilke wrote to her, saying that in 1915 Klee had shown him his sixty compositions, and adding:

I was attracted to and absorbed by them for many reasons, especially because they speak of Kairouan which I know. During the war years I often had this impression of watching objects disappear (because it is a question of faith, knowing up to what point we accept them, and how much we strive to express ourselves through them: in this latter case, perhaps broken beings are better represented by fragments, by the debris . . .) What is astonishing is that after the disappearance of the *object*, properly speaking, music and graphic art (drawing) assert themselves, reciprocally, as *subject* – this short-circuit of the arts behind nature's (or imagination's) back, this is, for me, the most disquieting phenomenon today, but it is also a liberating phenomenon: because one cannot really go further. And immediately afterwards (this, Klee would not accept, I fear), everything will be restored to order again.

This letter was a response to Merline's objections. She had not been convinced by Klee's work when she saw some reproductions in a book by Hausenstein. As we have just seen, Rilke himself was not entirely persuaded.

Franz Marc came back to see Klee during his short spells of leave. Klee played him some of Bach's fugues. Marc, less than comfortable in his lieutenant's uniform, listened, at the same time flicking through *Variations on a Landscape*, which Jawlensky had just finished painting in Switzerland. In March 1916, Klee was himself mobilized just a few days after hearing of Marc's death, in action at Verdun. Franz had been his dearest friend. Klee always thought of him with a kind of tender melancholy. They had many things in common. Even though Marc's approach to artistic creativity was entirely different, Klee had clearly defined what these differences were:

Marc is more human, he loves more warmly . . . there is something of the Faust in him, a need to be saved. Always asking questions. Is it true? He uses the word 'heresy'. But lacking the quiet assurance of faith . . . He has the feminine trait of wanting to share his treasures with everyone. The fact that not everyone followed him filled him with misgivings about his path . . .

Speaking of himself, Klee goes on:

I don't love animals and every sort of creature with an earthly warmth. I don't descend to them or raise them to myself (like Marc) . . . The earth-idea gives way to the world-idea . . . Everything Faustian is alien to me. I place myself at a remote starting point of creation, whence I state *a priori* formulas for men, beasts, plants, stones and the elements, and for all the whirling forces . . .

Military life for a territorial soldier even during the war wasn't so very awful. Klee was first sent to a *Rekurtendspot*, in Landshut (11th March–20th July 1916), then to the barracks in Munich (end of July–August 1916). Soon afterwards he was assigned to the Air Force in Schlessheim (August–December 1916), where he conscientiously painted aeroplane wings. He was also ordered to accompany convoys to Cologne, St-Quentin and Cuxhaven. Finally he was posted to Gersthofen, near Augsbourg, where a flying school was being built and where he became paymaster's aide. He managed to find time to paint, sometimes clandestinely, sometimes during his free moments. Some weeks before the end of the war, he was able to get a room of his own, but he still continued his paymaster's aide's duties. In his leisure time he read Chinese poets. He was granted leave to attend the opening of one of his exhibitions in Berlin, organized by Herwarth Walden, director of the *Der Sturm* gallery and review. Paul Klee was beginning to reap the rewards of his labour. His work was finding buyers and, with joy, he could now read the early reviews of his efforts, written by the poet Theodor Daübler, Adolf Behne and Wilhelm Hausenstein.

It was more encouraging still that, with the money he was beginning to earn, he could see the means of resolving financial difficulties at home. He could now be sure that, once demobilized and back in Munich, he would be able to engage a housekeeper and devote himself entirely to his work. He consequently saw increasingly little of Lily and young Felix. An important Leipzig weekly, the *Leipziger Illustrierte*, asked him to do some illustrations. Klee immediately wanted to know, 'Who will write the article? Which other artists will be collaborating? How much is the fee?' This was because, without being really interested, he had a kind of passion for accounts. This is perhaps the reason why he was entrusted with the regimental ledgers. Whatever the motivation, the sales figures he received from Walden and Goltz were appreciable. Rarely had even the greatest painters seen their earliest artistic successes so swiftly followed by finanical reward.

FIRST ASSESSMENT

'Creative Confession' appeared in 1920 in a small collective volume of texts by poets, dramatists, painters and musicians, also including Benn, Daübler, Unruh, Toller, Pechstein, Beckman and Marc de Schönberg. Klee had drafted a first version at the end of 1918, at Gersthofen, shortly before his demobilization. Jürg Spiller tells us that he entitled it, 'Reflections on drawing and on art in general', and that he had been inspired to write it by the recent publication of Kandinsky's essay, 'Painting as pure art'.

This text, the first Klee had presented for public consumption, began with this short sentence: 'Art does not reproduce the visible, it makes visible', thus condensing the reflections and experiences of twenty years of intense creativity. This formula encapsulates his aesthetic conceptions. He developed it like this:

Drawing, by its very nature, leads directly and quite naturally to abstraction ... The more a graphic work is pure, that is to say the more the accent is placed on the elements of form which are basic to graphic representation, the less one is able to represent visible things in a realistic manner.

We must examine Klee's extremely personal graphicism. 'The formal elements of drawing', he wrote, 'are the points, the energy of the line, of surface and space'. Klee tries to explain this somewhat obscure sentence by means of concrete examples. He suggests that the reader should accompany him on a country walk. Like this we will be able to see how natural phenomena can be represented by graphic signs and their combinations. We set off from a given point and we walk: this is the line. The line is interrupted, articulated. We cross a river in a boat: undulating movement. We come to a ploughed field: this is a surface scored with lines. There is fog in a valley: this is a spatial element. We meet people:

Basket weavers pass by on their cart (the wheel). With them there is a child who has interesting curly hair (helical movement); later the weather becomes heavy and overcast (spatial element). Lightning flashes on the horizon (zig-zag line). Above us, the stars (stippling).

The end of the day comes; we are back at the inn. And Klee, who must often have dreamt of walks like this in the Swiss countryside, or on the outskirts of Munich, concludes: 'Before going to sleep, we will remember many things because a little trip like this is rich in impressions.' He resumes:

Very different lines. Points. Smooth surfaces, speckled surfaces, striped surfaces. Undulating movement. Interrupted or articulated movement. Counter-movement. Interlaced or interwoven elements. Masonry, scales. With one voice, with several voices. Line which disappears, line which reinforces itself (dynamic).

The elements of an entire graphic vocabulary have thus been ennumerated and defined. But to obtain forms or objects, it will generally be necessary to combine several of these elements. It follows that: 'Thanks to such an enrichment of the symphony of forms, the possibilities of variation and, therefore, of expression are multiplied to infinity.'

Klee then goes on to study the essential relationships between the work and time (or movement). 'At the root of all becoming there is movement.' To begin with, he brushes aside the traditional distinction between the spatial and the temporal arts, a distinction formulated by Lessing in his *Laocoon* and one which Klee considered to be no more than a pedantic exercise, 'because space is also a temporal concept'. The elements of graphic representation multiply with duration: 'When a point becomes movement and line, this demands time. In the same way as when a line is displaced to produce a surface. And the same is true for movement which, starting from surfaces, can engender space.'

And the work itself? Its creation is subject to the same law: 'It is constructed piece by piece, like a house.' Reflecting on the birth of a work, the artist does not forget 'the other', the observer. 'And the observer, can he ever be finished with a single artist's work? (Alas, only too often.)' The serious observer needs time. This is why, 'Feuerbach said that a chair is indispensable in order to understand a painting. So that the mind is not distracted by tiredness in the legs.' Thus, always: time and movement; the indispensable and universal condition. 'The genesis of writing' is a really good image for movement. The work of art is, initially, genesis ... In the same way the spectator's activity is also temporal. Klee sums up his whole conception in a few words: 'A work of art is born of movement, it is the fixation of a movement, and is received by movement (occular muscles).'

Klee, *The Chariot of Virtue* (*In Memory of October 5th 1922*)

He continues:

Not so long ago, we depicted things we could see on earth, things we had, or would have had, the pleasure of seeing. Now what we show is the relativity of visible things. In doing this we are expressing the conviction that, in terms of the universe as a whole, the visible is only an isolated example and that other verities exist, latent and far more numerous'.

Klee then discusses the notion of good and evil. After the passage we have just quoted, he goes on:

Evil should not be an enemy which triumphs or confounds, but rather a force which converges in the realization of Everything. A factor which intervenes in generation and development. A simultaneity of the masculine principle (evil, stimulating, passionate) and the feminine (good, growing, patient), like a statement of ethical stability. This corresponds to the simultaneous combination of forms, movement, and movement in its inverse sense, or more naïvely, the combination of contrast of objects (in the realm of colouring, the use of colour oppositions as in Delaunay). Each energy demands a complement, to attain a perfect state of equilibrium . . .

Klee has taken us a long way down the road of abstraction and generalization. Finally coming back to earth, he chooses to give us some examples. The vision of ancient man corresponds to the experience of the early sailor on his boat; modern man, sailing on the bridge of a steamer, recognizes or is conscious of his own movement, that of the boat, the direction and speed of the current, the rotation of the earth, the course of the stars. The result is, 'an assemblage of movements in the universe, with the self aboard ship as centre'. Another example is as follows: an apple tree in flower is like 'an assemblage of states of growth'. A third example is: a sleeping man is 'an assemblage of functions united in rest'. In these cursory lines,

Klee gives away his secret, the mechanic of the image. The apple tree in blossom lives and grows before our eyes with 'its roots, the rising sap, the trunk which when cut reveals its age-rings, the blossom and its structure, its sexual functions, the fruit, the core and the pips'.

The liberation of elements and their regrouping, dissociation and reconstruction of the whole, the plastic polyphony, the conquest of stillness by the balance of movement; all these operations, analysed and recomposed in the art of artistic creation, are of vital importance to the understanding and the construction of forms:

But we are still not in the sphere of art in its highest form. In this highest sphere, behind the ambiguity, there is a final mystery. Art has a powerful effect on us, and through the imagination we recognize states of being by which we are stimulated far more than by any conscious state, be it earthly or unearthly. . . . Symbols console the mind.

With this vigorous and joyful appeal, Klee concludes his theory. He is inviting us to appreciate, almost like 'a healthy weekend in the country', the opportunity that art gives us to 'change our point of view in the same way as we might take a change of air'.

BABEL TO WEIMAR

In 1920, when the architect Walter Gropius summoned Klee to Weimar to join the newly-formed Bauhaus, Klee had already written 'Creative Confession'. The book was going to print with the publisher Reiss. 'Bauhaus' means 'house under construction'. Under this banner Gropius planned to unite a group of artists and craftsmen with the intention of giving birth to a new order, both artistic and ethical.

Klee in his studio in Weimar, 1924

Klee in his studio in Weimar, 1925

Gropius skilfully attracted able collaborators and backers: painters like Lyonel Feininger and Oskar Schlemmer; the Hungarian Moholy-Nagy; Georg Muche; the sculptor Gerhard Marcks and Meyer, the architect. Paul Klee, giving up his precious Munich, joined them in January 1921. Kandinsky, who, with his young wife, had returned from Moscow the year before, was the next to join the Bauhaus ranks, in 1922. The organization's manifesto was the underlying unification of all the diverse branches of art, and, above all, the harmonious amalgamation of craftsmanship and artistic creativity. Thus, the traditional division between fine and applied arts was eliminated: 'Our ultimate aim, still a long way off,' runs the first draft of the manifesto, 'is to achieve the unitary work of art, the Great Work which will nullify all distinction between monumental and decorative art'. This ambitious manifesto continues:

> Let us imagine, let us create together the new edifice of the future, which will be all at once: architecture, sculpture and painting, and which, born of the countless hands of craftsmen, will rise up towards the heavens like the symbol of a new faith.

In fact the Bauhaus was an advanced school of form and, as such, made its mark deeply on a period of polyvalent research, giving rise to the style whose name it bears and which, after so many years, remains intact. How did Kandinsky and Klee find themselves together under this banner? Today it is difficult to explain. It is not surprising that artists such as Kandinsky and Klee – both of whom had written about, and considered deeply, the problems of artistic creativity – should have agreed to teach at the Bauhaus. But neither the Russian's nor the German's plastic works have much in common with the communal spirit of Bauhaus, even though we can occasionally find affinities with their companions, notably Feininger. It is easier to comprehend the disagreements which existed between the artists inside the very temple of Bauhaus. These 'masters' were of widely differing temperaments. However, as the spirit of a school is formed by its adherents, Gropius's ideas and those of his faithful followers (doubtless also of Van Doesburg, who had arrived in 1921 to deliver lectures on neo-plasticism) put their stamp on the whole group. And however distinct and pronounced the characters of Kandinsky and Klee may have been, the two could not entirely escape the Bauhaus influence. There is no doubt that their own 'constructive' tendencies were heightened by it, and that such an active and strongly-directed milieu would have stimulated the development of their thinking, the extrapolation of their theories and their own dialectic. But neither artist completely submitted to the school's intellectual and aesthetic influence. For example, nowhere in the works of Klee, after his arrival in Weimar from Munich, can we remark a discernible rupture similar to the effect that cubism had on Picasso.

There is in existence a little text of Klee's which is extremely helpful to understanding the artist's way of thinking; it is to be found in a Bauhaus collective publication of 1923, entitled *Wege des Naturstudiums* (Study of Nature and its Ways). Here we rediscover the intimate, fervent tone of 'Creative Confession': 'Dialogue with nature remains a fundamental condition for the artist. The artist is a man, nature himself and a fragment of nature in the space of nature.' This axiom expresses a universal truth which remains constant, but what changes with the times are the methods employed in the study of nature, the essential condition of artistic creation. We must not be mistaken by the real nature of these innovations. 'The methods often seem quite new, without necessarily being so'. On this point, Klee's comments bear the mark of a prudent judgement, carefully weighed. 'We must not belittle the joy which the discovery of new ways affords us, but, on the other hand, a broad understanding of the past can save the artist from a convulsive search for novelty at the expense of the natural.'

What characterizes the artist of yesterday, in his relation to the palpable world, is:

a minutely differentiated examination of appearance. The me and the you, the artist and his object, sought, by means of the optico-physical, to establish a relationship across the layer of air which exists between the me and the you.

The positive result of such a system is that it gave us 'excellent images of the surface of the object'. The negative aspect is: 'The art of contemplating and revealing non-optical impressions and representations was neglected.' We should not therefore underestimate this conquest, which the understanding of the phenomenon represented, but neither should we remain satisfied with it. 'The artist of today is more than a perfectly constructed camera. He is distinctly more complicated, richer, vaster in scope.'

Our understanding of the object has been amplified and deepened. It no longer stops at appearance. It has gone beyond the limits 'things' put in the way of our tireless quest. More lucid, more adventurous, modern man is capable of dissecting the object and, with a dextrous incision here and there, can render the interior visible. What the eye apprehends is only the exterior aspect. Intuition penetrates far deeper into the secret heart of the phenomenon and makes a record of its marvels. Between the person and the object, the exchange of interrogations and responses provokes resonances altogether richer than the effects of simple optical sensation, because in some way it is the object itself which has thus become humanized, while the contemplator is entwined in the object, thanks to his oceanic sense of the universe and the intensity of his lived experience. For Klee, artistic creation implies a physical means of approach and a metaphysical function. Hear what he has to say: 'The lower path stops at the

domain of static forms, whilst the upper path gives access to the dynamic domain.' The formula would remain rather obscure, if he had not clarified his thought:

On the lower path, which passes through the centre of the earth, we have problems of static equilibrium, which we can characterize like this: staying upright in the face of everything that could make us fall over. We are led to the upper paths by the need to cut the ties which attach us to the earth, moving on, through swimming and flight, to complete freedom, to liberty of movement.

All paths meet in the eye and, transposed into form at their meeting point, they lead to the synthesis of exterior vision and internal contemplation . . .

Through the work in which he transforms the experience acquired on the different paths, the student indicates the degree of intimacy of his dialogue with nature. The more he progresses in the examination of this dialogue and in meditation, the more capable he is of arriving at a real conception of the world, and the more he will be able freely to create abstract compositions which, going beyond the arbitrary and the schematic, achieve a new nature, the nature of the work. He is thus creating a work, or, rather, he is participating in the realization of a work, which is an equivalent to the creation of God.

In his *Pädagogisches Skizzenbuch* (Book of Pedagogical Sketches) published in 1925, Klee addresses himself specifically to his students. This is a little scholastic manual which we will not discuss in these pages. If we assume that Klee was a conscientious teacher, we can be less sure that his doctrine was accessible to his whole audience. In the special number of the review *Du* dedicated to Klee in October 1947, one of his former pupils recalled that:

the extraordinary science of form that Klee had, of plastic means and their possibilities, allowed him to reveal in a short time to his students this magical power of the sign (unconscious in children but completely under control in Klee himself) which has always been the preoccupation of artists.

Nevertheless – if we are to believe the author of this article – the master's teachings lacked efficacy.

The formal elements so fine and so subtly invented by Klee engendered in his students only hollow imitations manifesting the product of an imagination out of control. What the students had drawn from their subconscious, they were incapable of combining with real data as their master did. Klee in fact was not only a great inventor, who tried to see the other side of things, he was also an observer and an extraordinary realist . . . But he alone had the head of Janus. He possessed another faculty which his students were able to exploit only within the narrowest of limitations, the faculty of turning the plastic means themselves into the content of a painting. He took, as point of departure, his graphic knowledge and gave his written or painted signs an original and new resonance. He never got lost in the vague or the indefinite, because when he composed his pictures he respected the laws, the laws which conformed to his own nature, and were thus intransmissible. His students, on the other hand, would lose themselves, and would at the same time lose the indispensable contact with the surrounding world . . .

THE PAINTINGS LOOK AT US

'The paintings look at us', Klee said at the famous lecture he gave in January 1924 during an exhibition of his work at Iena. The theoretician still has, within himself, a powerful antagonist: the mystic. To conciliate them, to unite them in creative effort: this was the course he tenaciously pursued right up to his death. The Iena conference was, in some ways, his *Discours de la Méthode*. Here, in the manner of Kandinsky, he deals with the most abstract aspects of the problems of creation. Published in 1945 under the title, *On Modern Art*, its reverberations were universal.

He begins with a confession: he would have preferred, above all, to consider the phases of the creative process as it develops in the subconscious, that is to say, to put the accent on the 'content' of the work. But that would have been to ignore the fact that most observers are more familiar with the content of the work than with its exterior aspect. And so he felt constrained to tackle the question of form. 'We are going to take a peek together at the painter's studio . . .'.

Klee continues:

All the same, there must certainly be common ground between artists and laymen, where it is possible for them to meet each other without the artist being considered as an exceptional phenomenon. The artist is a creature who, without being asked for his opinion, has been, like you, thrown into a confused world and who, like you, has to get along with it for better or worse. He is different in only one significant way: he resolves matters by his own means, and is, consequently, perhaps happier than the non-creator, who remains an outsider to all acts of real and liberating creation . . .

Allow me to make use of a parable, the parable of the tree. Take an artist, sufficiently well-orientated in the world and in life to be able to organize phenomena and experiences. This orientation of things in nature and in life, this complex organization with multiple ramifications, I would like to compare to the roots of a tree. From here, the sap mounts towards the artist, trying to pass through him, through him and his eye: he is thus taking on the function of the trunk. Urged on and

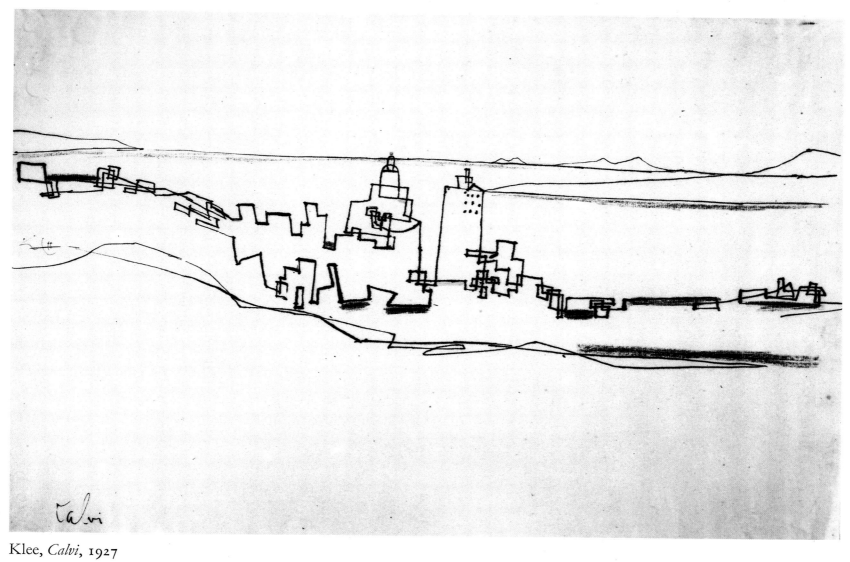

Klee, *Calvi*, 1927

Kandinsky and Klee in Dessau, 1930

Paul and Lily Klee in Dessau, 1933

agitated by this powerful flux, he transmits to his work what he has seen. And the work, like the top of the tree, unfurls into time and space. No one would demand that the tree should form its top in the image of its roots ... It is clear that, in different realms, diverse functions necessarily conclude in considerable differences. But we attempt to prevent the artist from shedding his models. We even accuse him of impotence or wilful falsification. But, like the tree, he is doing nothing other than gathering and transmitting forces welling up from the depths. Neither serving nor dominating, just transmitting. He has, therefore, an extremely modest function. He himself is not the beauty of the tree-top, he simply lets it pass through him ...

Let us now discuss the dimensions of the picture. In the work of art, nature is reborn, but necessarily deformed, submitted to the specific dimensions of the plastic work ... These dimensions are first of all formal elements, more or less limited, such as line, the values of light and shade, colour. Line is the simplest element, it is only a question of measurement ... Tonalities are of slightly different nature, the values of light and shade, the numerous gradations between black and white. With this second element we are dealing with a question of weight. A tone may be more or less charged with white energy, another with black energy ... Third element: colours. To arrive at an understanding of their nature, we can refer to neither measurement, nor weight. If we compare two surfaces, one pure yellow, the other pure red, the same size and of equal luminosity, there nevertheless exists a difference between them, designated by the words: 'yellow' and 'red' ... Colours, I would like to call them qualities.

These formal means, measurement, weight and quality, have certain relationships between them. Colour is, first of all, quality; secondly, weight, because not

only does it have a chromatic value, but also a value of luminosity; thirdly, it is measurement, because outside these previous qualities, it has its limits, its circumference, its extension, its measurability. The tonalities of light and shade are, first of all, weight, but also, in their extension and limitation, they are measurement. As for line, it is entirely measurement ...

Let us now go on to the first constructions done with the aid of the three categories of elements mentioned. It is here that we find the centre of gravity, the critical point of our conscious work ... If we are masters of our plastic means, we will be able to create forms capable of going further, touching on realms far vaster, and very distant from conscious experiences.

If, on the other hand, the orientation we stamp on form is insufficient:

the higher and more important contents cannot be attained and the finest dispositions of the soul cannot escape failure ... When such a composition is slowly developing before our eyes, we are easily tempted to interpret it in a figurative sense. Every unity of forms, whether more or less complex, can effectively, with a little imagination, be compared to things which are known and exist in nature.

And here we have the reason for 'these passionate misunderstandings which separate the artist from the public'. While the artist is completely involved in:

grouping formal elements in such a pure and logical way that each occupies the place to which it belongs without doing harm to its fellows, any layman, looking over the painter's shoulder, might pronounce the fatal words: 'But it doesn't look a bit like uncle.' The artist, if his nerves are strong, says to himself: 'Uncle or no uncle! I have to carry on constructing ... This new stone', he says to himself, 'is perhaps a little heavy, it puts too much weight on the left-hand side: I'll have to put a heavy counter-weight on the right, to keep the balance . . .' Sooner or later, however, and without any layman's intervention, an association (in the sense of an objective interpretation) might present itself to the artist's spirit and nothing will prevent him from accepting it if he considers it appropriate.

It is even possible that this could lead him to 'add this or that element which has a logical·rapport with the subject previously defined'. To the dimensions corresponding to elementary plastic means (line, tonality and colour), we should add, along with the constructive combination of elements, the dimension of organized form (Gestalt) or, if you like, the dimension of the object. There is one more dimension to add to these others, 'the dimension which corresponds to content'.

Klee goes into more detail: 'Certain relationships of magnitude in the lines, the juxtaposition of certain tonalities, certain concordances of colour bring with them clearly defined varieties of expression.' He gives an example:

Sharp zig-zag movements, opposed to a more horizontal linear trajectory, produce contrary resonances of expression . . . In the area of light and shade we find, with the extended use of tones, of black and white, expressive possibilities which convey force, inspiration and expiration, to which the use of the upper, lighter, half of the tonal ladder, or the use of the lower half, deep and dark, correspond . . . As for the possibilities of variation of content provided by colour-combinations, they are innumerable . . . And each organization of form, each combination will have its own constructive expression; each organized form, its face and its physiognomy. It is in this way that paintings look at us, serene or severe, tense or less tense, consoling or frightening, sad or smiling . . . But this is not all. These organized forms still have their particular 'attitude', which is a result of the way in which different groups of elements have been set in motion.

Klee then attempts to show how the artist arrives at an apparently arbitrary deformation of natural forms.

It is first that he does not accord these forms the crucial importance which the 'realists' gave them. In these 'finished forms' the artist does not see the essence of nature's creative process . . . He is, perhaps without knowing it, a philosopher . . . The deeper his eye penetrates things, the more he is forced to recognize, not an image of finished nature, but the only important image of creation: genesis. From this moment he believes he has the right to think that creation can hardly be achieved. He goes still further. 'This world had another aspect', he says to himself, 'and it will have another aspect.' And, over and above this, he permits himself to imagine that there exist, on other stars, entirely different forms. This mobility in the face of the natural ways of creation is a good school for the artist; it reaches down and touches the creator in his most hidden depths. And, as he is himself mobile, he will apply this mobility to his own plastic creations. Simply by looking in a microscope we can see things which would seem fantastic if, without having been warned, we came across them somewhere else by chance. Mr X, discovering a particular reproduction in some audacious review, would indignantly exclaim: 'Call this forms of nature? At its very best, it's bad industrial art!' [A little wickedness on Klee's part, as critics had employed exactly these terms in condemning his work.]

Is this to say that the artist must also make use of the microscope, of history, of palaeontology? Only as a point of comparison, only to become more mobile and more free, not scientifically to control reality . . . When we choose to copy, we must go back to the essence, to the principle of things . . .

Rare are the artists who are able to penetrate the secret depths where elemental law nourishes evolution and metamorphoses! What artist would not like to be at the organic centre of all temporal and spatial movement, the brain or the heart of creation which governs all functions, in nature's breast, where the secret key to all things is kept?

There is no single rule, however: let everyone go where their heart leads them. This is why the impressionists, our recent but antipodean neighbours, had the right to stand close up to the spectacle of nature, of daily life, practically at ground level. As for us, our heart takes us down into primordial depths . . .

However, all that the artist may bring back from his excursions into the depths, dream, idea, imagination, can be of value only if he is able to give it substantial form. In this way, the strangest of things become realities of art, making life fuller than it may ordinarily seem . . . In fact, it is in the domain of plastic resources where the birth of a painting is decided. Whether, indeed, it will be a painting or something else altogether. Further, it is here that the nature of the painting is decided. We live in disturbed and confused times, but there is a discernible trend amongst the artists of today towards a pure cultivation of the plastic means, towards a rigorousness and purity of use.

Klee is thus referring to the legend which had grown up around the alleged childishness in his drawing. But his intention was only to equate the representation of an object, or of a man, to the bringing into play of the pure linear element. An attempt at realist representation would have led to a convolution of lines so confused that it would have been impossible to speak of the purity of means. 'I don't want', said Klee, 'to represent man as he is, but as he could possibly be. This is how I have been able to align my conception of the world with a pure

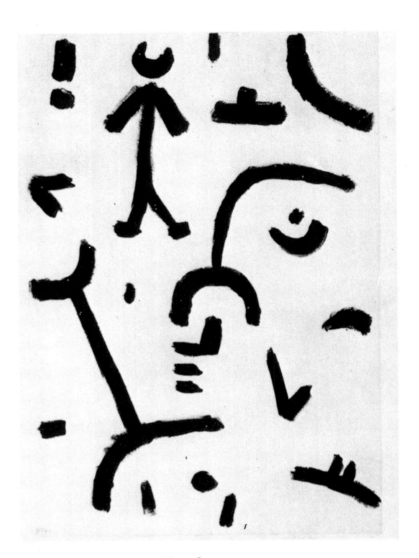

Klee, *The Child Just Went Out*, *1937*

artistic execution. In the whole world of plastic and coloured resources, we must avoid confusion and cloudiness.' As much as he worked on pure drawing, Klee practised all levels of painting: pure tonal painting, painting whose tonalities were charged with colour, the painting of complementary colours, multicolour painting and total chromaticism. Further, he tried all possible syntheses, all combinations, always maintaining, as far as he could, the cult of the pure element.

Sometimes I dream of a work of great scope, embracing the whole realm of the elementary, the object, content and style. This will certainly remain a dream, but it is a good idea to contemplate from time to time possibilities that are still vague today.

Klee, *Ah, but Ah!*, 1937

And, to conclude, it is still the artist speaking:
We must not rush into anything, we must let things mature ... We do not yet have this supreme force: a people to lean on. But we are seeking this people, we started it with the Bauhaus. We began with a community to whom we gave everything we had. We could do no more.

Raphaël, Dürer and Brueghel were supported by such a people. Today Picasso's dove flies round the world with its olive branch. But in 1924, behind Paul Klee and his friends, as behind Picasso and his enemies, there was only a small group of informed speculators and supporters. Isolated amongst his fellow men, often the object of hostility or, even worse, of indifference, the artist, in Klee's eyes, finds his true place in the face of nature to

which, in all its component parts, his work is bound. One could say about the Iena conference that it was a kind of declaration of artists' rights, not concerning the society of man but the community of things, at the very heart of the universe. 'Paintings look at us', but, in their expression, 'the artist is watching us'.

THE K.K. GESELLSCHAFT

In November 1925, Otto Ralfs, a modest businessman from Brunswick, a painting fanatic and collector in his spare time, was convinced by Klee's works the first time he saw them, as he would be soon afterwards by Kandinsky's. He had the idea of forming an association whose members would be able, by means of a small monthly contribution, to get hold of water-colours and paintings by both artists. This was the K. K. Gesellschaft.

Klee was then living in a villa in upper Weimar and Kandinsky in a little furnished apartment on the other side of the park. At the Bauhaus they had neighbouring studios. As in Munich, when they lived in the same street, they would see each other every day and often, in the evenings, they would get together with their wives at Klee's house or meet at the theatre. Kandinsky would sometimes invite his friend to go to the cinema, but only the name of Chaplin could persuade Klee to cross the threshold of a *salle obscure*. Even then he took only an indifferent pleasure in it. In the first days of Weimar, Klee sported a slight beard which, with his penetrating look, gave him the air of a character out of *The Burial of the Count of Orgaz*. Rolf Bürgi, accompanied by his mother, once went to see him. He retained the memory of a beautiful apartment, airy and light and full of antique furniture. The walls were covered with water-colours. A black cat, which terrorized Frau Kandinsky, reigned from the sofa. After the meal, Klee took his violin and, accompanied by his wife at the piano, began to play Bach and Mozart. The next morning they went together to the studio. As they were passing the outdoor theatre where Goethe had played the rôle of Orestes in *Iphegenia*, Klee amused his guests with a series of mimes, imitating attitudes for which the poet was famous: it was one of his favourite jokes. The studio made a strong impression on the young Bürgi, who described it as follows:

> One would have said it was an alchemist's laboratory. In the middle several easels and a stool. Klee worked simultaneously on many paintings ... He spoke with perfect simplicity: he had to do a certain thing, he said, in such a way so that the birds would sing.

In one of his water-colours of 1922 – which now hangs in the Museum of Modern Art in New York – he had invented the famous 'Twittering Machine'. Frau Bürgi wanted desperately to have 'The Bird Called Pep', a wonderful work done in transparent tones. The bird with his long pointed beak irresistibly called to mind the art-dealer Flechteim, a well-known gallery owner on the Lützowufer, in Berlin.

In 1926 the Bauhaus moved to Dessau, and the two Ks. found themselves in a village built by Gropius. Klee had seven rooms. Kandinsky, not being a father, had only four, but as his apartment was the first to be finished, Klee was for some time obliged to accept his friend's hospitality. Dessau was not a nice place to live. When Gropius summoned his teachers from the Bauhaus in Weimar, which had just dispersed, to discuss with Burgomaster Hesse the conditions under which the new school would be constituted, the women, who had come with their husbands, had discovered an old forest on the outskirts of the town. Since the municipality was unable to find them lodgings, why not trespass upon a little bit of nature? The Klees and the Kandinskys annexed a few

metres of extra terrain, providing them with small private gardens with no fence in between. But, as close as the two Ks. and their families were, it seemed as if there was an inviolable division between their respective domains. Klee would never set foot in Kandinsky's garden uninvited. And the latter would never infringe upon the limits set by the narrow border, defined on one side by Frau Lily's carnations and on the other by Frau Nina's roses. When they found themselves gardening, the two Ks. hardly spoke to each other, behaving as if they were each hidden behind the wall. And Nina Kandinsky, from the balcony above, looked on with surprise. Nina was a Russian from Moscow. She had lived in Russia during the Revolution. Such a scrupulous sense of individual property was alien to her. In truth, the two artists were behaving as if they were painting side by side, each absorbed in his own labour.

Frau Kandinsky has often spoken of these happy years, and the parties in each other's houses. The liveliest evenings were at her house. On one occasion Klee arrived dressed in a turban, showing off his oriental features. One would have thought that he had been born with this traditional head-gear of the magi and the maharajahs. The more intimate evenings, dedicated to music, took place at the Klees' house. These were simple meetings in the style of old Germany. Klee would revert to being a simple musician, completely taken over by Bach, Beethoven, Handel, Haydn and Mozart. Almost every night he would play, accompanied by his wife. They would then go to bed and read their favourite authors, Greek and French. But so absorbed was he in music that he would speak neither of poetry nor of painting. As the weather improved, they saw a little less of each other. Nina and her husband went on bicycle rides through the shady lanes. Klee and his wife were not really sporty types: Klee preferred walking. 'On foot you can see better,' he said.

Then came the summer holidays, and separation.

In 1924, Klee went to Sicily. In 1926, he returned to Italy; he visited Elba, Florence, Pisa and Ravenna. In 1927 and 1928, he travelled through France, Brittany and Corsica. In December 1928, he received some money from the K. K. Gesellschaft to pay for a trip to Egypt, where he stayed for just over a month. He did not take to picturesque Egypt with its mosques and market-places: it failed to meet his expectations. He only found the Egypt of his dreams in the pure geometrical lines of its monuments, the flowing sand and water, in the pale light of the colour-saturated sky. This is the Egypt which would remain one of the themes most deeply etched in Klee's sensibility.

During 1928, growing problems within the Bauhaus forced the resignation of its founder, Walter Gropius. He was briefly and unsuccessfully replaced by Hannes Meyer. From 1930 up to its closure by the Nazis in 1933, Mies Van der Rohe took charge of its destiny. Klee's situation seems to have been affected adversely by these events. The current problems and their repercussions on the status of the Bauhaus painters caused Klee to write to his friend and biographer, Will Grohmann, in a letter dated 15th September 1928: 'How distressing it is, after each holiday, to begin again in Dessau. We no longer know why we teach, and even the painting isn't going so well.' Klee left the Bauhaus in 1931 for the School of Fine Art in Düsseldorf, to take charge of an arts course.

THE RETURN TO BERN

In December 1933, fleeing from Germany, Klee sought refuge in Bern. Unexpectedly, he arrived on the doorstep of his friend Bürgi: 'I'm back,' he told him, 'there's no place for me any more in Germany.' Although he had been exhibited in New York and Paris and his fame was henceforth secured, few people in his home town had even heard of him. Frau Bürgi went to great lengths to get him better known and admired. Will Grohmann was invited to talk about Klee's work in Bern.

Klee had been forced to leave everything behind. Dismissed from the Düsseldorf academy, there were even moments when he feared for his life. Lily, who had no illusions about the Hitler regime, had been pressing to leave for a long time. In the end Klee was resigned to the idea. Distant was the time when he could write in his *Diary*: 'Without Germany, what would become of me?' But here was Klee in Bern, disillusioned, sad, dispossessed, but not without support. Rolf Bürgi himself went to Düsseldorf to fetch the works Klee had left behind in his studio. Frau Klee was displaying unprecedented, attentive devotion, for she was no longer the authoritarian Lily of yesteryear. Now convinced of her husband's genius, she showered him with almost reverent affection and loving care.

Would Will Grohmann succeed in convincing the Bernese of the immense value of Klee's work? Whatever was to happen, Frau Bürgi's generous initiative was producing some results. She was the first of her compatriots to have complete faith in the artist, at a time when the ageing Hans Klee was still sceptical. 'I don't say that he has no talent,' the old man would grumble into his long beard, 'but he doesn't bring enough conviction to what he is doing'. While some of the Bernese began to be convinced, the city authorities remained deaf to the eloquence and erudition of Klee's biographer. But Klee was quick to understand that he would never return to Germany. He decided to ask for Swiss nationality. This step provoked the usual mistrust that artists can expect from the upright bourgeoisie. A town councillor vehemently opposed Klee's application, alleging to have

Klee in Bern, 1938

seen a work by the artist which was gravely offensive to Switzerland. The work in question depicted a little meadow into which too many dairy cows had been herded. 'This proscript's art is damaging to us', he complained. 'He would have the whole world believe we don't have enough pasture for our cattle.'

Perhaps this was nothing more than a quirk of Bernese humour. Even so, some years before, Arp had filed a similar request which met with a no less surprising response: 'Your craziness will lead you to the madhouse. And it is us who will have to provide for your upkeep, and the medical attention your condition will require.' Arp did not insist. Klee, however, was more tenacious and he persevered. He was finally granted Swiss nationality seven years after his return to Bern. It came too late; he died the day before, and died a German.

When he took refuge in Bern, Klee was 54 years old and still felt in robust good health. It was only three years later, in 1936, that he began to have doubts whether his constitution could withstand the disease which would finally take him away. Nevertheless, his flight from Germany had left him severely shaken. This country had given him everything and he wanted to give it his all in return. He had become, in fact, thoroughly German. But this new Germany was rejecting him, a Germany which condemned his work as 'degenerate art', a Germany which allowed a hundred of his compositions to be seized by the Nazis.

As he had done in Weimar, Klee began to examine his conscience. He made his own evaluation; he questioned himself. He asked himself if he had really achieved the goals he had set himself. In so doing, he submitted his earthly frame to brusque punishment. After a bout of measles, he contracted a skin disease which dried up his mucous glands. He could only swallow liquids, and those only with the greatest of difficulty. It was not an unusual complaint in Europe, but a spirit as imaginative as Klee's could fear it as much as any mysterious tropical disease or witch-doctor's curse. It was hardly a simple coincidence, then, that in his drawings his line lost some of its assurance and adventurousness. Undoubtedly it still responded to the artist's will, but it lacked the capricious delicacy of old. Klee's creative faculty was now concentrated on 'signs', which had 'a semantic value like Chinese characters in the *Book of Changes*'.

In 1937 and 1938, Klee at last took on the large surfaces which he had always dreamed of. He mixed glue and plaster to prepare his canvas. He alternated smooth and rough surfaces and threw together canvas, cardboard, wrapping-paper and newspapers. He used all painting techniques at the same time: oils, distemper, water-colours and, most often of all, pastels, for their softness.

The linear expressionism of 1937 and 1938 gave way to the figurative expressionism of 1939 and 1940, with angels and demons in a treatment at once crude and refined, revealing the anguish Klee was going through as he approached death. He could feel it coming. He even had to give up the carriage rides which Rolf Bürgi used to coax him into taking. During 1939, on the second floor of a little villa in Kistlerweg, in the embassy district, Klee's output was prolific.

That summer Kandinsky came to see him. Two years before, Braque and Picasso had paid their respective visits. Kandinsky found his friend in bed. By way of encouragement, he invited him to come to Paris. From his sick-bed, Klee sketched a little gesture of doubt in the air without moving his head from the pillow. His expression seemed to say: 'We will never see each other again.'

In February 1940, just a few months before his death, Klee agreed to have his work exhibited in the Zürich Kunsthaus. The critical reaction was negative in the extreme.

Carola Giedion-Welcker tells us:

When I saw Paul Klee for the last time in his Bern apartment, I felt in him, despite his habitual calm and impassivity, a certain agitation inside. He spoke to me about this outburst in the Swiss press. The big Kunsthaus exhibition, the ripe harvest of seven years in Bern, had provoked all sorts of attacks and misunderstandings. This hostility seemed to arise from the fact that the painter of detail (as he would always be considered) was expressing himself in a monumental language of rare austerity and astonishing force.

Nowadays, it is hard to imagine the extent to which Klee's art could, in 1940, through its inspiration and style, irritate certain critics. One detractor even went so far as to hint at schizophrenia.

One day in May 1940, Klee seemed to be exasperated by the press critics, who were having, he feared, a dangerous effect on his life in Switzerland, hindering or, at least compromising, his chances of becoming naturalized. I only became aware of this when I unthinkingly suggested that such vulgar allusions to an intellectual anomaly, designed to entertain the public, could in no way intrude upon his internal life, because I was only considering the situation from the point of view of a real compassion. Klee simply commented, in a dry manner, that this suspicion of schizophrenia would hardly encourage the authorities to grant his residence papers. Klee, who was to die some weeks later in Locarno-Muralto, was right. His mother's country and the country of his youth, the country whose language he spoke – even when he lived in Germany, he spoke only authentic Bernese – was never to become officially his homeland.

On 10th May, shortly after Carola Giedion-Welcker's visit, sensing the end approaching, Klee asked his wife to accompany him to the sanatorium at Orselina, just above Locarno. Some months earlier the artist's old father had died, and Paul had said to Lily: 'You will see that I won't outlive him by long.' His condition was worsening daily. On 8th June he was rushed to the St-Agnes clinic in Muralto-Locarno. Paralysis had reached his heart. So as not to cloud his last moments, no one mentioned the war. The German offensive and the fall of Paris were kept from him. On 29th June, his heart stopped.

His cremation took place in Lugano on 1st July. On 4th July, in the chapel of the Hopital des Bourgeois in Bern, a funeral ceremony was attended by, alongside Klee's wife, several of his friends: Hermann Rupf, Rolf Bürgi, Hans Bloesch, Hans Meyer-Benteli, Werner Allenbach and Georg Schmidt, the curator of the Basel museum. Felix was not there. He had seen his father for the last time at the end of the year before, when he talked extensively about Sicily, where he had just been with his wife, Efrossina. He was now in the forces, somewhere in Germany.

Hans Bloesch and the cathedral pastor both spoke. Then came the turn of Georg Schmidt:

Amidst the clamour of so many deaths, the most silent, the most exceptional artist of today has passed noiselessly away. For a long time now, those near to him trembled for this precious life ... I have seen Klee's last works. Difficult though it is to say, there is no trace of the buds of a new springtime. They are the 'finale' of a life, consciously ebbing away. To say it with more precision, more truthfully and with heightened grief, they are a variation on the theme: full stop.

In September 1942, the urn was transferred to the Schlosshalde cemetery in Bern, not far from the Bentiger quarry where the artist often went to draw when he was still a young man. White and yellow asters, begonias and roses decorate the tombstone on which the epitaph is an extract from the *Diaries*: 'Here below, I am unreachable. I live as much with the dead as with those who are not yet born. A little nearer to the heart of creation than usual. But still not as near as I should be.'

Klee in Bern, 1939

THE PLATES

Garden Scene with Watering-can, 1905

Klee had been established in Bern since his return from Italy in 1902. Notes from his *Diaries* reveal a double dissatisfaction with his lot: Bern bored him and his work was progressing too slowly. He was going through an internal crisis of self-doubt. In spite of the undoubted originality of the 'severe style' etchings, he was intensively seeking an outlet that would lead to his mastery of colour. The move from etchings to *sous-verre* painting marks an important stage in his artistic career.

In a letter to Lily written in October 1905, there is at last a ray of hope. By accident, he had discovered a technique for painting on glass. The group of works produced in this manner (fifty-seven in all) gave Klee the opportunity directly to attack the problem of colour. The procedure is painstakingly recorded in his *Diaries*. First he covers the glass plate with a coat of white. Once dry, this layer is scratched with a sharp point to create the motif. Colours are then applied to the scratched areas. When finished, the plate is reversed and the motif appears *sous-verre*.

Most of the *sous-verre* rework, in a less inhibited fashion, the grotesque or satirical 'invented' motifs of the earlier etchings. Hence the importance of *Garden Scene with Watering-Can*, a unique example of a liberating process moving towards luminosity in painting. This was the actual starting point for the difficult conquest of colour only to be fully realized in 1913–14. In his *Diaries*, Klee finally declared himself satisfied with his progress. In a letter to Lily, he made a reference to his stay in Paris the year before, where he witnessed, for the first time, the luminous clarity of the impressionists.

Young Girl with Pitchers, 1910

Klee was gradually becoming familiar with French painting. In 1909, he saw eight Cézanne pictures at the Sezession exhibition. 'This is the master "par excellence" ', he noted immediately in his *Diaries*. *Still Life with Four Apples*, in the New York Museum of Modern Art, is an example of the assimilation of the principal characteristics of Cézanne's style. Similarly, we can see traces in *Young Girl with Pitchers*, painted the following year. The folding table-top, perfectly coinciding with the painting's perspective, recalls the technique much used by Cézanne in his still lifes.

On the other hand, in the first-ever monographs on Klee, written in 1920, Hausenstein and Zahn pointed out distinct similarities between this picture and the work of Matisse. There had indeed been a Matisse exhibition at the Thannhauser gallery in February 1910. Klee makes no direct reference to it in his *Diaries*.

But in April 1910, he offered this description of his most recent work, which corresponds to the letter to *Young Girl with Pitchers*:

New assault on the fortress of the 'painting'. First the preparation of the background with white, thinned down with linseed oil. Then, lightly colour the whole surface, especially with large patches of different colours which blend into each other, remaining free of all chiaroscuro intention. Third, the drawing; independent of all the rest, a kind of ersatz tonal valorization. Finally, a few bass notes to prevent any flabbiness, not sombre these basses, but brightly coloured.

It is a combination of drawing and colouring, a way to maintain my fundamental graphic capacity, while moving into the domain of painting. (*Diaries*)

In choosing this path, Klee was directing himself towards the progressive recognition of the autonomy of colours. No longer do colours merely describe objects: they make up an harmonious accord between themselves, and, further, they serve to engender a space without depth. The two parallel lines which replace the relief of the nose also serve to emphasize the flatness of the basic materials. We think immediately of Matisse's painting of 1905: *The Green Line (Portrait of Mme Matisse)*.

Kairouan (Departure), 1914

Kairouan was the last place visited in a two-week trip to Tunisia in April 1914, in the company of the painters August Macke and Louis Moilliet. During his stay, Klee did a series of water-colours which would represent for him the assimilation of all he had discovered from discussions and encounters over the preceding years.

Without a doubt, it is to Robert Delaunay that Klee owes his understanding of the spatializing function of colour. But the light and tonalities he discovered in Tunisia had a determining impact on the later evolution of his painting. In his *Diaries* there is a detailed account of the different stages which led him to pronounce: '. . . colour and I are as one. I am a painter'. It was at Kairouan itself that he made this declaration.

'In the morning, facing the town, I painted in a delicately dispersed light which was both clear and gentle.' This attention to subtleties of nuance goes hand in hand with a desire for structuring: 'I launched an attack on the architecture of the city and the architecture of the painting.' The water-colours done *in situ* show that the realization of this task was by no means an easy one. Here Klee is attempting to create space with colour-schemes, using the white of the paper as a background for transparent effect. The oblique lines in the foreground convey the immensity of the desert surrounding the town. By the use of delicate graphicism, he conjures on to the horizon the surrounding wall of the town, the domes and several mosques. In fact, these water-colours are 'notes' to which Klee would refer the following summer in his increasingly abstract chequered compositions.

Klee

1914. 42. Kairuan

Motif from Hamammet, 1914

Back in Munich, Klee set about exploiting his Tunisian experience to the full.

For someone whose main preoccupation was drawing, this new mastery of colour held the promise of unimaginable possibilities. At last Klee too was able to construct pictorial space by means of colour organization.

The irregular grill constituted by the juxtaposition of rectangles and squares recalls *Fenêtres sur la Ville*, which Klee must have seen in Delaunay's studio in 1912. But the functioning of space in depth is distinct from the Frenchman's technique, and even from the Tunisian water-colours, which provided the departure point for these compositions.

In fact, in this little oil painting, Klee completely reverses the process through which he obtains his final result. Instead of placing transparent tones in flat tints on a white background, he places semi-opaque tones and textures on a dark background.

He maximizes his depth of space by placing a red triangle on the bottom right and a blue rectangle on the top left. The tension thus created sets up a complex and ambiguous space, constantly at play with the eye of the spectator. Certain lighter configurations seem to be advancing; the darker ones recede, whilst the half-tints facilitate the movement between background and foreground. Contrary to what is suggested by the hill in the foreground and the vegetal motif on top of it, we have here a purely abstract construction which has no origin whatsoever in nature.

The discreet mobility of the figures is wholly congruous with the notes Klee made in his *Diaries* at this same period: 'Ingres, it is said, tried to organize stillness; beyond pathos, I would like to organize movement (the new romanticism).' Klee from then on was moving towards an extremely personalized form of abstraction, which distinguished him from both the expressionists and the Dadaists. His position regarding the war which was to break out in August 1914 was one of distancing himself, not to be confused with a straightforward escape from reality.

Kakendaemonisch, 1916

1916, a year when destiny played its part. At the beginning of January, Louis Moilliet's wife died giving birth to a baby boy, her first-born. On 4th March, my friend Franz Marc was killed in action at Verdun. On 11th March, I was called up as a 35-year-old reservist. (*Diaries*)

Being mobilized caused no great interruption to Klee's work as he still found time to draw and paint. The works produced were fewer in number, but, nevertheless, the diversity of the series begun in this period, the quality of invention and the technical innovations by means of which they were accomplished indicate a real progression. In *Kakendaemonisch*, Klee introduces a new process: he paints the water-colour on canvas prepared with plaster and mounted on cardboard. This mixing of techniques gives him access to previously unobtainable textural effects. It represents a real breakthrough in his quest to solve creative problems which will characterize all his future works.

Alongside the *Miniature* series and the water-colours inspired by Chinese poems, another group stands out, thanks to the association of a complex iconography with the formal research on which he was already embarked. In *Demon above the Ships* and *Introducing the Miracle*, indefinable beings, half-angel, half-devil, perfectly integrated into the arrangement of the colour schemes, look obliquely out from the picture, never fixing the observer's eye. We find this look again in *Kakendaemonisch*: two ocular motifs are integrated in a geometrically designed structure.

As J. Glaesemer judiciously points out, *Kakendaemonisch* comes from the Greek *kako-daemonia*, meaning 'possession by an evil spirit'. By introducing the simultaneous presence of good and evil in his work, Klee underlines his interest in the relationship of opposites, both formally and semantically. He says in his *Diaries*: 'The diabolical raises its ugly head from time to time and cannot be repressed. Truth necessitates all elements at once.' The titles of his paintings are an integral part of the works. Klee is using them here to multiply levels of meaning and to echo the general state of conflict represented by the war.

Coloured Angles, 1917

Seeking to achieve greater mobility in his work, Klee carried out a series of purely formal experiments using angles. A network of parallels and interlocking angles creates a density in the picture, in which certain features recede and others seem to be pushing outward. The ambiguity of perspective thus achieved forces our viewpoint into continuous movement. Having mastered the use of formal abstract elements, Klee later employed the same technique in rather more ambitious compositions.

Ab Ovo, 1917

This little painting is classified 'Category Apart' in the catalogue of work Klee conscientiously maintained. This was how he would designate those pieces he deemed sufficiently important to make a special note of. 1917 was a year of intense activity, during which his pictorial output was matched by theoretical statements on a theme already begun in 1914: 'Genesis as formal movement constitutes the essence of the work' (*Diaries*)

These theories were a development concomitant upon a profound self-examination provoked by the death of his friend Franz Marc. Klee sought better to define his position in terms of being an artist. He came to the conclusion that, 'The passionate ways of humanity are doubtless lacking in my art . . . In me, the earthly gives way to cosmic thought.' The romantic consonance of this affirmation perfectly shows his desire to present an image of himself as the 'outsider', allowing him to keep things at a distance. 'I occupy a distanced, original creative position, from which I transmit a priori formulas for man, animal, vegetable and mineral . . .' There are several reasons why Klee favoured this image of himself: economic (according to Werckmeister), strategic and ideological (according to Geelhaar) and aesthetic (according to Glaesemer).

The same could be said to apply to *Ab Ovo*. The image of the egg was, for Klee, a visualization of the founding principle of his theory of art: that of 'formal genesis'. On a background of incandescent light (achieved by means of a chalk preparation) a central structure unfolds where cosmic and organic motifs overlap. Darker-coloured triangles, pointing to the centre, occupy the periphery and enclose the composition. They force the eye to concentrate on the horizontal axis. Ovoid and angular forms cling to the background which supports them. They communicate with it and between themselves by the subtle interplay of transparencies.

This painting is remarkable because of the quality of integration of elements into the totality of the work. The balance of tensions between opposites, light and dark, curve and angle, achieves an undeniable perfection. The strength of this functional unity in the work of art is analogous to the workings of an organism, an analogy which Klee was to take up and insist upon in his Bauhaus courses from 1921 onwards. The presence of the heart shape at the centre of this composition makes it virtually a painting-manifesto.

Harbour at Night, 1917

Continuing his research into chalk-based painting, Klee produced, between 1917 and 1918, several 'nocturnal landscapes'. These landscapes display common characteristics and recurrent motifs, demonstrating the vast scope of Klee's network of cultural references, from which the motifs were drawn. We have examined elsewhere the correspondences between certain Klee images and Chinese poetry. But James Smith Pierce has drawn up a comprehensive inventory of motifs borrowed from the traditions of popular art. Like Kandinsky, Klee was familiar with the schematic painting of Bavarian peasants. Since 1912, he had been using the full spectrum of celestial symbols such as the sun, moon, quarter-moon, six-pointed star and asterisk.

The problem in interpreting these symbols is that when Klee turned them into images, he transformed them into formal elements and personal symbols which are often difficult to decipher. The symbolic value changes from one work to another, creating a displacement of meaning. The signification of a Klee image is almost always multiple, and the best means of approaching it is to proceed by comparisons.

In several works of 1917, the boat motif constitutes a kind of metonym for the war: *Boat Alert, Sketch for the Evil Star of boats* and *R. Mi* (*Navy*). Elsewhere, a mountain landscape may symbolize a specific location. In order to propose an interpretation, we must consider the ideological context in which such images were produced. The war was far from creating unanimity, and amongst the entourage of collaborators on *Der Sturm* (the review and the gallery where Klee was frequently exhibited), pacifist reactions were emerging, seeking to review the decadent values which had brought Germany to the brink of disaster. By using a simple graphicism with its overtones of childhood drawings and a reconstruction of formal elements which he had made his own, was not Klee simply proposing a departure towards a better world?

Under a Black Star, 1918

In the context of general disillusionment at the end of the war, a number of pacifist writers, such as Kornfeld, Toller, Rubiner and Klabund, tried to group artists together to engage in a 'saviour' mission. This mission, however, was not intended to instigate direct social action. It was more a question of the artist 'transforming himself' and then re-presenting himself as model. This ideology of regeneration, inspired by Chinese thinking, was present in German thought up until the early 1920s.

There exist in Klee numerous configurations of this new conception of the artist as 'saint' or 'prophet'. In 1918, two works put forward this theme: *Predestined Boy* and *Agnus Dei qui Tollis Peccata Mundi*. In each, Klee presents a frontal view of a personage spreading his arms in a gesture of prayer.

As in the works previously mentioned, the figurine 'under a black star' is placed beneath the form of an arch, suggested by the dark arc to the left, completed by four circular forms in pink. The arch is a recurring element in the landscapes of 1918, as is the star. The function of these figures is always to denote a mystical place where the relationship between things is subject to other laws.

In a work dated 1916 and called *Destruction and Hope*, the six-pointed star appears in the foreground, superimposed on a chaos of tangled lines. Two years later, Klee takes up this symbol of hope again and integrates it into a mountain landscape strewn with stars, the sign of a new Messianic era for many writers of the same period. These crosses reappear again in 1918, in a landscape heavily inspired by Chinese thought, entitled *Hermitage*. The combination of the cross and the hermetic wisdom of the Chinese allows Klee to convey a twofold sense of regeneration. The exceptional number of works he sold in 1917 and 1918 bears witness to the pertinence and topicality of his subject.

Composition with Windows (Composition with the letter B), 1919

In February 1919, Klee was finally demobilized. He rented a studio in the little castle of Suresnes in Munich, and committed himself to a more systematic study of paintings in oil. He signed a three-year contract with the Goltz gallery and finished his first theoretical essay: 'Creative Confession', to be published in Berlin in 1920.

Composition with Windows is another painting classified as 'Category Apart'. It comes from an important series of landscapes in which the artist re-examines, in order to further clarify, the problem of movement in painting. Using, once again, a basic structure of a grill made up of different sized rectangles, he gives to the theme of the window (for which he is indebted to Delaunay) a wholly personal interpretation.

Whereas in Delaunay's picture the window takes up the whole surface of the canvas, in Klee's we see it divided and multiplied with its cross-bars and curtains into little basic units spread all over the surface. These units are then bound to a network of colour-schemes. The whole surface thus divided takes on the multiple connotations of a rhythmic facade or of a terraced architecture, to which he adds a few vegetal elements. By means of a subtle interplay between dark configurations which seem to be retreating and lighter ones which appear to advance, he creates an interior/exterior opposition on the surface.

We should not approach any of Klee's works as if it were a set representation of the world. Our vision must accept the visual tensions which set the work in motion for the eye of the observer. The movement here is punctuated by enigmatic black signs: the letter B, an exclamation point, a triangle. Their form is perfectly integrated into the whole of the composition. But their precise meaning escapes us. In a passage from 'Creative Confession', Klee explains:

> Arising from formal abstract elements, going beyond the associations they produce as concrete entities or as abstract objects like numbers or letters, a cosmos of forms is finally created, so similar to the great act of creation itself that it is only a breath away from the transformation of religious expression into religion in action.

The symbolic landscapes painted since 1917 do indeed contain this dual expression of the formal and the spiritual, usually conveying the sense of Utopian regeneration.

Perspective of an Occupied Room, 1921

At the end of 1920, Klee was asked by Walter Gropius to join his team of teachers at the Weimar Bauhaus. The courses he was consequently obliged to draft give us precious insight into his objectives and his conception of movement in painting. The works he produced during this teaching period are not simply the practical application of the grand principles analysed in his classes. The opposite was more often the case; as he says in a letter to his wife in 1921: 'Here in the studio I am working on half a dozen paintings, I am drawing and, at the same time, I am thinking about my courses. Because everything must work together, or it will not work at all.'

Klee increasingly sought to bind linear structural tension with coloured space. To this end, he perfected an original and complex technique which enabled him to transfer a drawing on to another sheet which had previously been covered with colours. Between the two he would slide a third sheet coated with a thin layer of black oil paint and then go over the outlines of the drawing with a metal point. The accidental patches caused by the pressure of his hand provided an additional textural element. This method of working was the basis for a great number of works during the Weimar period. *Perspective of an Occupied Room* is an example.

The elaboration of formal rules was the principal axis of his teaching at Weimar. For the benefit of his students, Klee re-embarked on an examination of the laws of perspective, taking advantage of this to develop a new conception of space. Structure 'seen in perspective' is open from all sides. Recession in space is opposed to a contrary, circular movement, suggested by the oval form of the borders. The perspective is thus transformed into one of floating, uncertain space creating a reversal of the stability associated with classical space perspective.

This work might have been nothing more than a fanciful demonstration of the laws of perspective. It is necessary, however, to place it in the broader context of Klee's output. In 1921, Weimar was subjected to repeated attacks by Theo Van Doesburg, editor of the Dutch review *De Stijl*. Since 1919, he had been publishing a series of articles overtly criticizing expressionist tendencies at the Bauhaus. An associate of Mondrian and of the architect Oud, he was the instigator of a radical new approach to creativity, based on the purification of means of expression. Depending exclusively on perspective and straight line, they sought to suppress, in painting and in architecture, the individual for the good of the collective. *Occupied Room* functions as an ironic commentary on the excesses of such an exclusion for the sake of a 'law' applied too rigidly. Klee forces his characters to bend before the 'laws' of perspective, to the point of being flattened against walls or ceilings, eternally subordinated to the structure. In other words, when the law is stronger than the individual, the human figures no longer exist in space, they are mere inhabitants of a perspective.

K. N. The Smith, 1922

In a text published at the Bauhaus in 1923, 'Different Paths in the Study of Nature', Klee credits the artist with a privileged position in the overall scheme of things.

> The artist of today is no longer a simple photographic device, however perfected; he is more complex, broader and richer. He is a creature of the earth, and a creature of the universe, a creature on a star amongst stars.

As usual he is speaking the language of analogy and metaphor. To further clarify his thesis, he accompanies his text with a diagram in which the artist is seen at the centre of a global totality consisting not just of the world of daily appearances, but also of the 'terrestrial' and the 'cosmic' from which he should draw his inspiration. The 'paths' of creation:

> establish between the Me and the Object a resonant relationship which goes beyond the optical starting-point. First, the non-optical path of common terrestrial roots, which inside the Me rises up to the eye; secondly, the non-optical path of cosmic unity, which asserts itself from above. The fusion of metaphysical paths.

The smith is clearly a prototype of the artist himself. His profession is traditionally linked to the transformation of metals. The great mythical narratives accorded him the power to organize the world. The forge itself, designed for the working of metals extracted from the earth, is associated with subterranean fires. Possibly Klee chose to call him K. N. as a kind of cryptogram, taking two letters from the word *'Kunstler'* (artist).

There are indications that the image of the smith reflects the image Klee had of himself as artist. Not only is he at the centre of the composition, but he is an integral part of the two clearly demarcated scenes. His structure and that of the anvil open out to space from every angle. The lower members melt into the 'earth' element. An upper member literally disappears into the canvas. The application of a red/orange denotes the incandescence of fire. A red arrow points towards whatever is being drawn from the 'earth'. A second curved arrow, making up part of the structure of the anvil, points to the artist's eye. The third, broken arrow points the eye in the direction of the 'cosmic' plan.

Klee made abundant use of the arrow in his explanatory diagrams in order to illustrate his theories of form. 'The arrow represents the displacement process and expresses deployment in space.' Transposed from the pedagogical diagram to the work of art, the arrow must be integrated in terms of form. In *K. N. the Smith*, it contributes to the integration of the figure into the background. Klee achieves this integration through the intimate linking of the arrows to the 'anvil–smith' structure, by means of pen-strokes. Here we have the clearest expression of his conception of the artist.

Fragment from a Ballet for the Aeolian Harp, 1922

Klee's intimate relationship with music has been mentioned time and time again. The son of a family of musicians, he himself played the violin. He was a great opera lover, and a love of ballet and theatre too. From the age of 10, he regularly attended concerts. Sometimes his works would allude to one of these events, such as *The Vocal Material of the Singer Rosa Silber*, 1922, and *The Singer L. in the Role of Fiordiligi*, 1923. But in most of these cases, as the work would be titled only after completion, the title was more a free association with memories than a direct allusion to one particular scene.

Fragment from a Ballet, on the other hand, is a testament to the quality of exchange between the Bauhaus teachers. The theatre workshop was very active, and the creation of masks and puppets was central to their research into presenting the human form in a different guise. Klee's work abounds with puppet figures with their visible articulation and their wooden gestures. Here, the neck and arms articulated with rivets clearly indicate the nature of this 'dancer'. The triangular form of the legs, the clearly exaggerated hips and the disproportionate size of the head recall the costume drawings done by Oskar Schlemmer, in the same year, for his *Triadisches Ballett*. These figurines could also be a reference to the automatons created by Lothar Schreyer for his theatrical production *Der Mensch* in 1921. The presence of the curtain on the left of the picture confirms the theatrical character of this work.

In the early 1920s, Klee frequently used the world of puppets and automatons to express his more general view of the tragi-comic side of certain human situations. Here, in humourous mood, he puts a fragile character on stage who looks more than likely to be blown away by a wind emanating from the 'aeolian harp'.

The Twittering Machine, 1922

A fragile drawing appears on a gently modulating coloured field by means of the oil-transfer technique. Simply amusing perhaps, at first sight, the 'machine' merits closer examination. A quartet of birds is perched on a branch; this in turn is attached to a crank-shaft, linked to a curious apparatus which looks like some kind of mirrored bird-trap, consisting of a stem and two triangles resting on four feet. A pink rectangle with feet gives the impression of a gaping hole or ditch, thanks to a judiciously placed vertical in the upper right-hand corner.

The first bird on the right has been pierced through the head by an arrow, its neighbour through the body, and the third through the eye. Only the last bird on the left seems to have survived this hecatomb. Its tongue takes the form of an exclamation mark, a danger-sign in Klee's iconography.

A. Kagan has convincingly shown that another work of the same year, *The Chariot of Virtue* (*in Memory of 5th October 1922*), in which the birds are replaced by four little characters, contains autobiographical elements. The date in brackets indicates that this work owes its origins to specific events taking place at the Bauhaus in the autumn of 1922. In fact, the ambiance had become strained owing to conflicts of opinion between Gropius and the other teachers. We know that Klee was less than appreciative of these internal squabbles and that his biting humour could soon turn against the protagonists. This sense of humour, which allowed him to distance himself from events, provides the basis for a considerable number of works, and is not always apparent on first viewing.

The Twittering Machine reworks several elements from *The Chariot of Virtue*: the four figures, the arrows, the presence of a little 'machine'. It is perfectly plausible to conclude that what we have here is a parody of the situation in which the Bauhaus teachers found themselves at this time. Klee created a graphic transcription of the current conflicts, their effect on individuals and the fate that awaited them. A simple turn of the crank-shaft would be fatal.

This work takes its place in a complete series produced in 1922, in which Klee, as the detached observer, made ironic comments on many subjects which affected his personal life, as in *Dance Monster to my Soft Song* and *Contact of Two Musicians*.

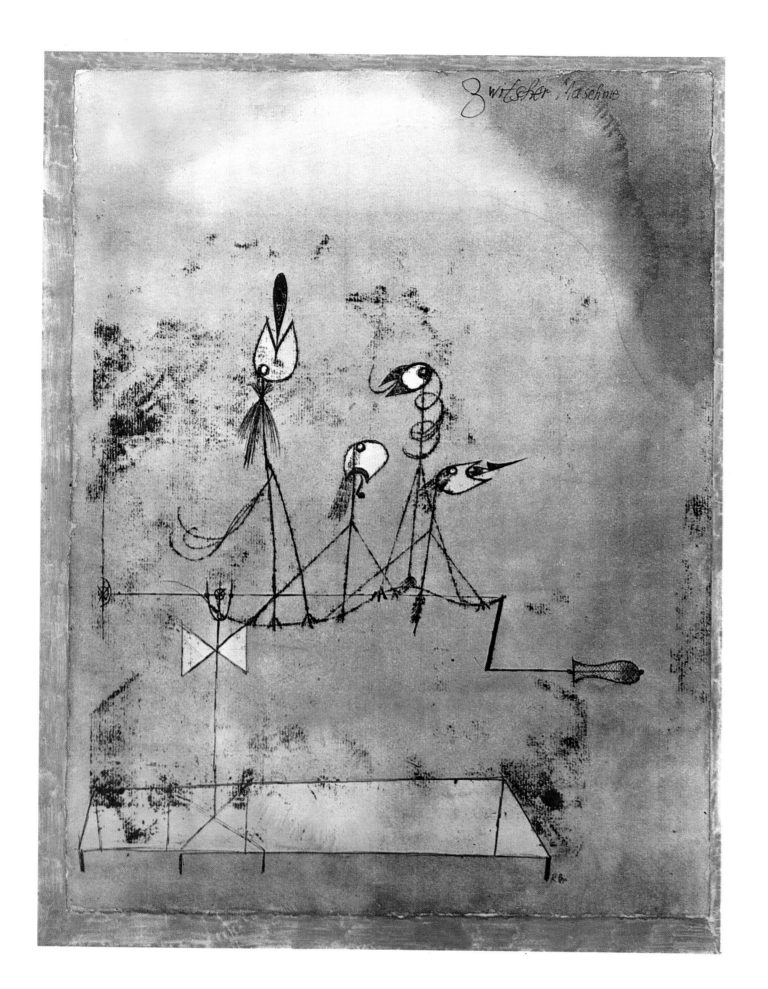

Senecio (Soon an Old Man), 1922

Ever since *Menacing Head*, in the series of etchings we know as the 'severe style' of 1904, studies in physiognomy had been one of Klee's preferred ways of presenting, in his inimitable humorous fashion, the panoply of human emotions. The solemnity of *Senecio* sets it apart from the others. The first impression we get is that a 'presence' is at work.

Many theories have been offered to interpret this enigmatic personage. This fact in itself underlines the typical polyvalence of meaning which characterizes Klee's most successful works. Unfortunately these theories rarely take into account the double title of this work. Titles, we know, play an integral part in the understanding of Klee's works. They always contain a clue to an interpretation of the iconography. For its part, the painting has to contain the visual references necessary for its proper understanding.

Whatever the point of reference for *Senecio* may be, one should emphasize the extraordinary mastery of purely formal means responsible for its creation. Klee manages to establish both the abstract and the figurative and keep them in a state of tension. The force of this image derives from the fact that it is not limited to a form on a background. The face is expanding in the space of the painting, space created entirely by the energy of colour. There are subtle interruptions in the contours, ensuring an exchange between the face and its background. The flatened nose can be seen frontally or in profile. The slight displacement of the red eyes, mobile colour *par excellence*, supported by the green arch of the eyebrow, coaxes our vision into a rotating, leftward movement, corresponding to the perfect circularity of the head.

The difference in form between the two eyebrow arches suggests the make-up of the tragic clown. The white recalls Pierrot's traditionally powdered face. The subtle coming and going between the frontal view and the profile seems to be a visualization of the passing of youth into age.

Theatrical and circus characters frequently appear in Klee's work. Already, in 1912, he had drawn *Head of Young Pierrot*, sad and melancholy. The first production of Schonberg's *Pierrot Lunaire*, in the same year, was noted by Klee in his *Diaries* as a major event. Two water-colours of 1923 depict *Pierrot Prisoner* and *Harlequin on the Bridge*. The recurrence of the image proves that Klee's intention is rather more than a simple diversion. Here Klee, in the manner of Picasso or Rouault, is presenting a veritable 'portrait of the artist as saltimbanque', perhaps even a 'transvestite self-portrait'. If we consider *Senecio* in terms of Jean Starobinski's penetrating analysis of clowns, the real significance of the image is clear:

> ... the choice of the clown image is not simply a selection of a pictorial or poetic motif, but an oblique and parodizing way of posing the question of art. Since romanticism ..., the buffoon, the saltimbanque and the clown have been hyperbolic and wilfully 'deformed' images that artists have chosen to give of themselves, and of the artistic condition.

For Klee to depict himself 'soon to be old' is certainly a thinly veiled statement of his position as artist at the heart of the Bauhaus, in the face of the irreversible rise of a formalist conception of art.

Eros, 1923

In this water-colour, Klee takes us far from the familiar image in Hellenist and Roman art, of the young boy, the mischievous winged tempter with his bow and arrow. Even if we look at it from the point of view of erotic content, recurrent in his work either satirically (*Adventure of a Young Girl,* 1922) or grotesquely (*Woman and Beast,* 1904), we are in the presence of a new proposition rather than a simple variant. Klee is trying to produce, this time, an equivalent in pure form to the power of universal attraction.

This work is a part of the series of water-colours in 'chromatic gradations' which he began on his arrival at the Bauhaus in 1921, envisaging the systematic exploration of colour theory which he was to expound to his students.

Amongst the works in this series, *Eros* continues the research begun in *Salutation* (1922), *Evening Separation* (1922) and *Double Tent* (1923), with the aim of visualizing two contrary movements, working principally with the power of graduated complementary colours. These gradations are set into a rigorous construction of horizontal strips. On to the horizontal layout of *Eros*, triangular forms are superimposed, created at first sight, by the intersection of oblique lines.

In one of his courses, Klee explained the genesis and formation of the three basic forms: triangle, circle and square. The vocabulary employed is essentially dynamic, attempting to explain how to create tension between pictorial elements necessary to the genesis of forms. A sentence extracted from this course may facilitate an understanding of the layers of meaning at work in this picture: 'The triangle is formed in the following manner: a point establishes a relationship of tension with a line and realizes this relationship by following the order of its Eros.' By introducing here, 'its Eros', Klee, for pedagogical purposes, is creating a metaphor, a transfer of meaning from the biological to the pictorial. This water-colour, *Eros*, is attempting to 'make visible' such a transfer. The interaction of the triangles is superimposed by the action of two arrows, one indicating the direction of 'the attraction' and the other the point of contact with the small red triangle, source/origin of the whole process. The stepped layers between the biological and pictorial order are central to Klee's teachings and to his theory of creation.

1923. 115. EROS

Aimiable Look, 1923

As of 1923, in parallel with his teaching on the movement of colour, Klee was developing his check structures, composed of rectangles and squares within which tone combinations could evolve. Using once more the structure of the Tunisian water-colours, he now confronts a different way of juxtaposing colours according to subtle gradations. We should note that he is composing with abstract unities, no longer with nature-based impressions. However, working in oils, he could not achieve the same transparent effects. He was obliged, therefore, to invent a new technique to convey a sense of depth. *Aimiable Look* is one of the first of a long series of non-figurative paintings, which he continued up to the 1930s.

The colours are applied to a dark brown and black background which constitutes the tonal base to which each colour must accord. In his classes, Klee complained that the triangle of colours could not take into account variations in tonality. He also wanted to go beyond the space configuration of the chromatic circle. In order that all the possibilities of colour movement should be realized, he introduced the use of a chromatic sphere, the centre of which is grey and the two poles black and white. Klee attributes greatest depth to the black, which is furthest from white on the central axis of luminous values. Thus, he always begins his checkered compositions with a dark tone, then works with superimposed layers in the direction of the lightest. The colours are positioned in a supple checker-board, whose elements are not rectilinear. By means of a slight tilt to the vertical, Klee introduces a subtle play of diagonals assuring the sedate mobility of the whole, in a way which induces a rhythm into our perception, in perfect time with the rhythm of expansion from centre to periphery.

The title *Aimiable Look* is a good example of a designation bearing no identifiable relation to the painting. With this simple allusion, Klee is tipping a wink to his public, inviting them to be led along 'the organized pathways of a work of art' ('Creative Confession').

Child on the Steps, 1923

The pictorial space is immediately recognizable as a *Marchenlandschaft* (fairy-tale landscape) reflecting the romantic cultural background from which Klee drew a large part of his inspiration. The fairy-tale form is hardly new. The romantic poets used it in order to transmit, in their particular way, a belief in supernatural forces at work in the very heart of the 'real'. Magic and mystery are at the heart of the tale of Kingsohr in Novalis's novel, *Henry of Ofterdingen*. They are also present in *The Golden Vase* by E. T. A. Hoffmann and *Egbert the Blond* by Tieck, creating the general climate in which the action takes place. These tales also make use of popular beliefs and folklore, which gives them their charming naïve quality.

What is depicted here is certainly not the content of a particular tale. Klee is instead alluding to the ambiance of the stories, multipying the graphic signs of the trees and the cottages in an extremely mobile space, an invitation to take a walk with him. A figure of a child is moving towards a series of lines arranged like a staircase, leading to the centre of the image, where we find the form of a little castle with a barely discernible, almost hidden door. The unreal aspect is reinforced by the choice of colours. The 'scumbled' application serves to translate the hazy nature of a landscape under fog. The positioning of white and yellow patches forces the eye to scan the picture to discover the different elements of this landscape as they appear and disappear.

Landscape with Yellow Birds, 1923

Beneath this apparently childlike and playful image is hidden the re-emergence of a thematic element often to be found in Klee's work at the end of the war. This kind of fantastical landscape resplendent with birds was extremely successful with the public, for whom the images evoked the gardens described in the tales of Novalis and E. T. A. Hoffmann.

Here, Klee's intention is to present a cleverly constructed recombination of elements. W. Kersten has pointed out that this composition was produced by the 'cut-up' process. Klee often used this procedure, aiming to destabilize the general harmony of things and to make its meaning more enigmatic. Originally, the motif of the purple-red arborescent plant was in the centre. After the cut-up process, the two sides were reversed and reglued on to card, leaving a space between them. This strip was painted in order to match the black background of the water-colour. It introduces a new centre to the composition. Klee added two yellow birds to the strip with the dual intention of drawing attention to the cut-up (the bird cut in two) and of re-creating unity with the circular arrangement of yellow points.

Carnival in the Mountains, 1924

Without being an exact pictorial transcription of a tale by Hoffmann, the night scene in *Carnival in the Mountains* nevertheless produces the same effect of disquieting strangeness. Two masked figures, led by a great bird recalling the ostriches in *Princess Brambilla*, are transfixed with amazement before a kind of automaton running into view, an hallucinatory figure, a construction of peculiar elements, brandishing an ocular shape. Other ocular forms punctuate this composition. Geelhaar suggests a connection with the Sandman, who, according to legend, tore out the eyes of children in order to sell them. Whether or not this is true, the attitude of the protagonists in this mysterious scene manages to evoke a feeling somewhere between the marvellous and the terrifying.

Klee's most complex images remain largely unexplained. We have always known of his passion for the opera. Glaesemer draws attention to a little-known fact, pointing out Klee's great interest in Offenbach's operetta, *Tales of Hoffmann*, in which he asututely perceived the hidden tragic dimension. A drama of puppets and automatons, this image is probably a disguised representation of the human drama, 'in the manner of Hoffmann'.

In 1924, the Bauhaus was experiencing serious political difficulties which gave rise to financial ones, eventually leading to its closure at Weimar. After some months of prospecting, Gropius moved students and teachers to the town of Dessau, which gave them a generous welcome. Gropius went quickly back to work, and the new building, in a style wholly suited to the needs of the school, opened its doors in December 1926.

Since 1923, Klee had been pursuing his research into the constructive possibilities of colours in a series of works accomplished periodically, at irregular intervals, up until 1936.

Ancient Sonority is a highly developed work in terms of the possibilities of articulation of space in a painting. The light-coloured rectangles begin a movement from left to right, a movement which, nevertheless, seems to be slowed down in its development. In fact, these light colours are emerging from a dark background from which they cannot detach themselves. They are 'held back' by this background whose presence we are always aware of, in spite of the opacity of the pigment. All the space of the painting is invoked by a double movement in surface and in depth, black being, for Klee, the expression of greatest depth.

The title functions, as a clue might, to refer us to a meaning which is diffuse and, doubtless, multiple. We can elucidate, perhaps, with an analogy with music. Here we know that Klee preferred, above all, the eighteenth century – Bach and Mozart. But this title could just as well refer to a chiaroscuro painting and the richness of tonal possibilities contained within it.

We believe, moreover, that this work contains Klee's ultimate reply to the aesthetic of *De Stijl*, whose basic principles were already being shaken by the controversy between Mondrian and Van Doesburg. The latter sought to break with orthogonal purism by introducing a diagonal into his compositions. Always keeping his distance from these tensions, Klee proposed another way, by which he showed that it was still possible to convey 'universal values' in painting without submitting to the purification of pictorial means which *De Stijl* proposed. His ways showed that one can explore different forms of abstraction/construction without submitting to the narrow limits of dogmatism.

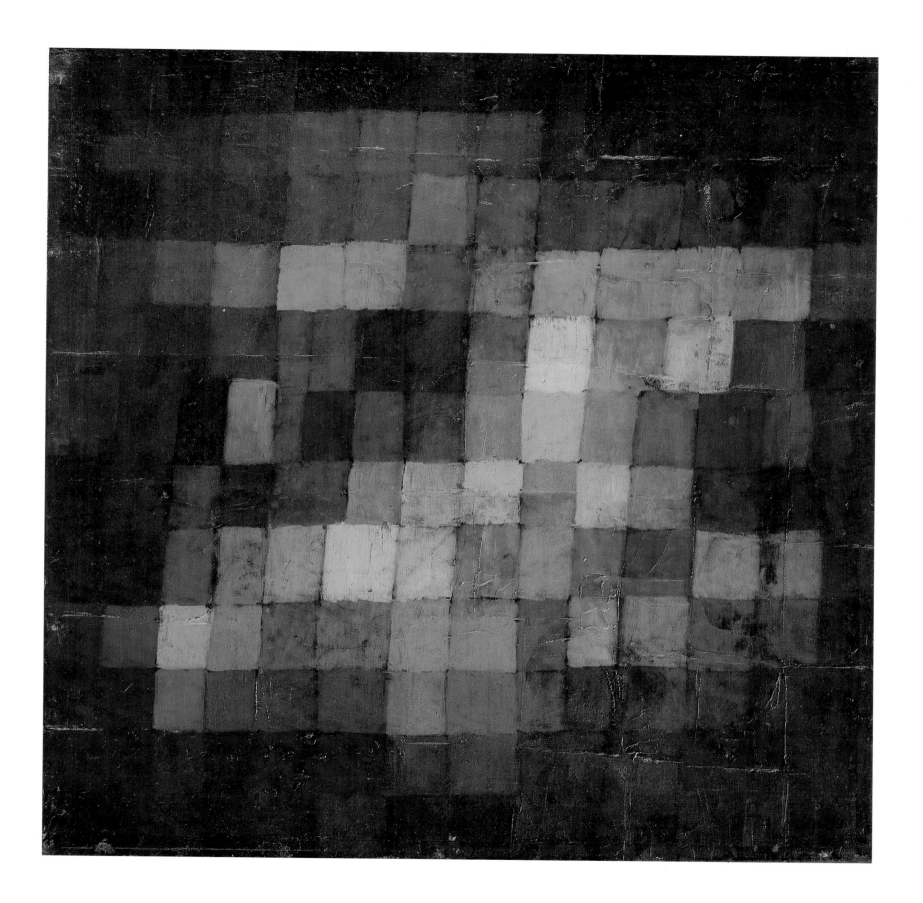

Florentine Villas, 1926

Klee had already been interested in different forms of calligraphy and their invention. Hieroglyphics, pictograms and ideograms captivated him, as much for their semantic as for their structural value. Since the very first abstract drawings of 1913, he had progressively built up a repertoire of signs and pictograms which he constantly reused, varying the context of their presentation. *Florentine Villas* belongs to a veritable series of structural compositions spanning the five years between 1924 and 1929. The faded pinks and ochres are certainly the origin of the title. Space is constructed by a subtle association of two structures: one is composed of irregular rectangles recalling the Tunisian water-colours, the other of parallel horizontal strips which constitute the basic structure of this series. The signs, sometimes etched, sometimes drawn, are organized non-symmetrically. The rhythmic distribution of the abstract motifs and pictograms on the surface alternates with the evocation of the facades and staircases in the background. Klee thus achieves a synthesis of structures in flat projection, with structures which are open to different perspective viewpoints.

Coast of Provence 6, 1927

From 1924 on, Klee spent his holidays travelling towards the light of the South. He first went to Sicily, then in 1926 to the isle of Elba, to Pisa, Florence and Ravenna. In August 1927, he spent some time on the isle of Porquerolles, then he embarked for Corsica. During these trips he would work *in situ*. On his return home, he would begin a series of works taking up, in the form of reminiscences, the motifs collected during his voyage. The transformation which these motifs underwent would often provide the basic structure for a whole series.

'The dialogue with nature remains a condition *sine qua non*', he wrote the following year in a polemical text published at the Bauhaus. Confronted with the new orientation which the teaching was taking in order to accentuate the production in series of functional objects, Klee maintained a firm position in favour of a personal pictorial method. If the development of formal laws constitutes the principal access of his teaching, he did not abandon, for all that, research into the passage which leads these formal laws to the work itself, assuring its dynamic character.

Inspiration renewed by his stay in Porquerolles, he set out to find a graphic transcription which would allow him to convey both the luminosity and the rhythm of this pleasure port. To obtain the effect he wanted, Klee used a triple system which, when simultaneously perceived, confers to the surface the mobility desired. By means of a linear system, rectangular and triangular surfaces spring up, interlocked one with the other. These surfaces are animated with an internal rhythm by the inscription of strips of pure colour which constitute a second system. The combination of these systems is registered on to the background by the addition of a structure of very subtle colour schemes. The surfaces are animated by the repetition of tight little brush-strokes, which transmits to the pictorial design the intensity and finesse of a vibrant luminosity.

1927 X 4

Côte de Provence 6

Chosen Site, 1927

After several weeks in Porquerolles, Klee continued his vacation in Corsica. He went to Calvi and Bastia, then to Corte and Ajaccio. The letters he wrote to his wife reveal the strength of the impression this country evoked in him. He declared himself profoundly touched by its 'heroic', even 'enigmatic', character, more so than by the delicate colours of Porquerolles. Two water-colours painted in 1927 find their origin in one or other of two particularly remarkable locations on this trip: *Chosen Site* and *City on Two Hills*. Comparison with a drawing he did in Calvi perfectly explains the transformation which Klee made from the original motifs to the finished work.

Starting from a point faithful to the original drawing, he brings to the surface a profile of the old city by means of knotted lines and overlapping designs. The moon motif, this 'southern moon', which has reappeared periodically in his paintings ever since his trip to Tunisia, occupies a strategic position, providing balance to the composition, as the town motif slants slightly from left to right. Its structure corresponds to that of the town, creating a tension between the two motifs, as if one were a detached fragment of the other. Both structures are painted with a fragile luminous density.

The most astonishing thing about this work is the background, divided into areas of saturated colour. The blue strip at the bottom of the composition denotes water; a transitional orange strip offers access to the reddish-brown of the earth. Then an immense green area progressively spreads into an equally dense red, giving a special effect to the whole, an effect which in itself succeeds in translating the 'enigmatic' character of the original location.

1927 X.8.   ausgewählte Stätte

Highways and Byways, 1929

Klee's trip to Egypt in 1928 was, for him, the realization of one of his dearest dreams. It was also the opportunity to take in a landscape and geography whose characteristics would play an integral part in the transcriptions he made the following year.

The basic structure consists of horizontal strips of stratified colours. Klee varies the length of these strata by introducing verticals or diagonals at irregular intervals. In this way, he effects a reorganization of his basic structure, progressively moving towards a purely formal arrangement.

For its part, *Highways and Byways* owes a lot to the Egyptian terrain. Two structures overlap to produce a pictorial equivalent of the principal and secondary routes leading from the fertile plains to the Nile, traversing the strip of desert, allowing us to view them from the upper plateaux. Varying the angle of the diagonals, Klee gives direction to his two routes, independent of his arrow, simply by formal arrangement. He creates waves, not steps, thus giving the impression of sand dunes. The central strip gives a strong impression of flatness. It recedes into a distance which itself seems to be approaching us, as we perceive that the blue and mauve strips at the top of the picture are in the same plane as all the others, and, especially, in the same plane as the blue strip at the bottom of the picture.

These light tones are to be found in all the water-colours Klee did on his return from Egypt. Clearly, for Klee, they best translate the actual light of that country.

Before the Snow, 1929

In January 1928, Walter Gropius resigned from the Bauhaus after nine years of director-ship. Hannes Meyer, who had Marxist leanings, was nominated as his successor. Klee was to remain for two more years at the Bauhaus, in spite of growing ideological tensions which were disturbing personal relationships. The near-polemical tone of a text Klee wrote in the same year for the Bauhaus trimestrial review demonstrates the evident dissatisfaction with which he viewed the school's options. 'Exact Experimentation in the Realm of Art' reiterates the great principles of his teaching, opposing them to a conception of art that was too technocentric. Exactitude and precision in research cannot replace intuition but should always go hand in hand with it.

The next year saw the appearance of a series of water-colours which Grohmann was to call 'atmospheric creations', in which Klee sought to translate into the pictorial dimension meteorological phenomena – *Mixed Weather* and *Atmospheric Group in Movement* – and growth phenomena – *Illuminated Leaf* and *The Twins' Place*.

Before the Snow presents an isolated motif in a landscape of sombre and menacing colours. The theme of the solitary tree in a vast landscape, victim of a hostile climate, is common to romantic painting of the beginning of the nineteenth century, particularly in the work of C. D. Friedrich, who generally sought to invoke a state of empathetic communication with a nature subject to the cyclic unfolding of the seasons.

Klee wanted to go one step further and show that which normally escapes our vision: the internal aspect of transformation in the natural elements. This is why he presents irregular constructions, with strong organic connotations, seen in section. These constructions either interlock, or are reorganized by an internal linear schema which is 'arborescent' and dynamic. He thus creates a tension between a growth factor and a stability factor provided by the horizontals of the landscape. This water-colour attempts to unify his previous research into the interpretation of organic growth and atmospheric perturbations.

Individualized Measurement of the Strata, 1930

During the course of 1929, Klee continued his research into the organization of surface by means of horizontal strips of colour. Several water-colours and two important paintings, *In the Current, Six Rapids* and *Fire at Evening* show Klee's interest in this very abstract form of constructive articulation.

Individualized Measurement of the Strata is a variation on *Fire at Evening*, and seems to be the last in the series. It is classified as 'Category Apart', indicating that Klee considered it a particularly successful work. As Glaesemer pointed out, the distribution of the surface is not arbitrary. It depends on two precise numerical relationships. The work is divided into twelve horizontal strips, in turn subdivided by five verticals. In this way, numerous irregular surfaces are created, animated by the artist by means of his colour distribution, always avoiding the static, reaching for the dynamic, as he would reaffirm over and over in his courses.

The black background which appears in the periphery and is visible behind certain pink strips is an example of the same procedure he experimented with in *Ancient Sonorities* in 1925. In the present case he brings to play a rapport between thin and thick coats of pigments, introducing a subtle textural play to a structure which would otherwise be extremely rigid.

Rythmical, 1930

During his last year of teaching at the Dessau Bauhaus, Klee returned to check structures to produce an austere and reduced series of works. This group finds itself isolated in the ensemble of his output. Here he gives, once and for all, a visual realization of his notions of rhythm which he ceaselessly expounded in his classes. Perhaps his aim was to provide his students with concrete examples. This would explain why they were less painstakingly completed, using pastels with glue, worked with a knife. Whatever the case, the structure of these works mimics, more than any others, an elementary musical structure. In his classes, Klee often compared the scale of tonal values, from black to white passing through all gradations of grey, with a musical scale (or scale of sounds), but pointed out that, 'any scale is already an artificial structure, an artificially fixed rhythm'.

In a work like *Rhythmical* we are, on the contrary, in the presence of what Klee called a 'superior structure', in the domain of chiaroscuro, which elevates us above and beyond the simple 'scale structure'. To present the image of such a structure, the normal arrangement must undergo a fundamental modification. To achieve this, Klee proposes, 'to cut the scale in two, in such a fashion that the division leaps out at us . . . The black and the white clash against each other in brutal contrast', whilst the passage from grey to white is rather more progressive. The values he uses are here thus reduced to three.

But, as Grohmann had already seen, 'the ternary rhythm suppresses the chess-board character, turning the sketch into a musical moment'. We could say rather that the occasional interruption of the ternary rhythm, by the omission of a colour at the end of a line, introduces a variation into the basic rhythm. The association in the same plan of irregular rectangles and a varied rhythm, which deconstructs the graduated scale, produces a sensation of pulsation in the eye.

Gleiten (Slipping/Floating), 1930

Between 1930 and 1932 Klee produced several compositions consisting of designs and volumes floating in a state of weightlessness in an indeterminate space. *Hovering (About to Take Off)*, *Floating Town* and *Having to Rise* present delicate structures intended to be the pictorial equivalent of 'pure dynamic', the principles of which Klee attempted to explain in his classes. The visual effect created by these constructions corresponds point by point to an example of mobile space already proposed at the time of an exhibition in 1924:

> A lightly oscillating structure entirely suspended between surface and background, possessing neither top nor bottom, but turning slowly on itself, which can if need be present a kind of centre to the internal construction, but for the rest, obeys a law which is purely dynamic.

Gleiten reapproaches structures made up of rectangles, squares and irregular polygons. These designs are transparent, opaque, stippled or striped, and are connected to each other by an 'illogical' linear network, making for the indeterminate volume of the floating object. But unlike the works mentioned above, the central object is placed in an apparently confined inner space. It is equipped with a plumb-line which maintains its balance and keeps it suspended. To the left, a polyhedral hexagonal, the volume of which is underlined by surfaces moving from light to dark, seems to be slipping slightly to the right. To make things clearer, we should note that the verb '*gleiten*' has two meanings: to slide and to hover. In this way Klee visually unites, in the same image, the two senses of the verb. The angle formed at the meeting-point of the ground and the walls serves not only to introduce contradictory points of view, but also allows us to perceive that the circle and the volume on the left are also in a state of weightlessness.

A series of drawings with the title, *Model*, accompanies this group of paintings. They are studies of very complex geometric figures, by means of which Klee explored new possibilities of creating movement, bringing to mind the research done by his colleague Moholy-Nagy.

Ad Parnassum, 1932

Faced with the progressive rationalization of the work and the extremely politicized ambiance at Bauhaus, Klee had become silent and retiring. From 1930 he requested the termination of his contract with the establishment; this was granted in April 1931. He was consequently free to accept a post offered by the Dusseldorf academy, where he could at last restrict his teaching exclusively to painting.

As we can observe, Klee simultaneously pursued very different kinds of research into structures: in checks, horizontal strips, suspension, etc. The Dusseldorf period gave him the opportunity more thoroughly to develop a series of 'polyphonic' paintings, begun in 1930. He had foreseen the possibility as long before as 1918, as he admitted in an entry in his *Diaries* concerning the painting of Delaunay: 'Polyphonic painting is in this sense superior to music, in that the temporal is more spatial. In it the notion of simultaneity reveals itself even more richly.'

Andrew Kagan maintains that the title of the painting is a disguised quotation from a treatise on counterpoint written by the Austrian composer Johann Joseph Fux in 1725: 'Gradus ad Parnassum'.

Using his concept of polyphony, Klee intended his paintings to correspond with a multivoiced musical composition. On a technical level, he made this visual analogy by superimposing a succession of tightly grouped dots of different colours and intensity on to a background structure of checks. He was thus using the divisionist system in painting which he had employed to convey vibrations of light in the Porquerolles water-colours. The fluctuating field of colour produced by this technique allowed Klee to create effects of depth without having to revert to traditional artifices. He also arrived at subtle transitions between light and shade, which depend essentially on the use of complementaries.

This painting is the largest format used by Klee to date. Was he indicating that this work represented a kind of recapitulation? Or did he simply consider that he had achieved a high degree of perfection in this system of transcription?

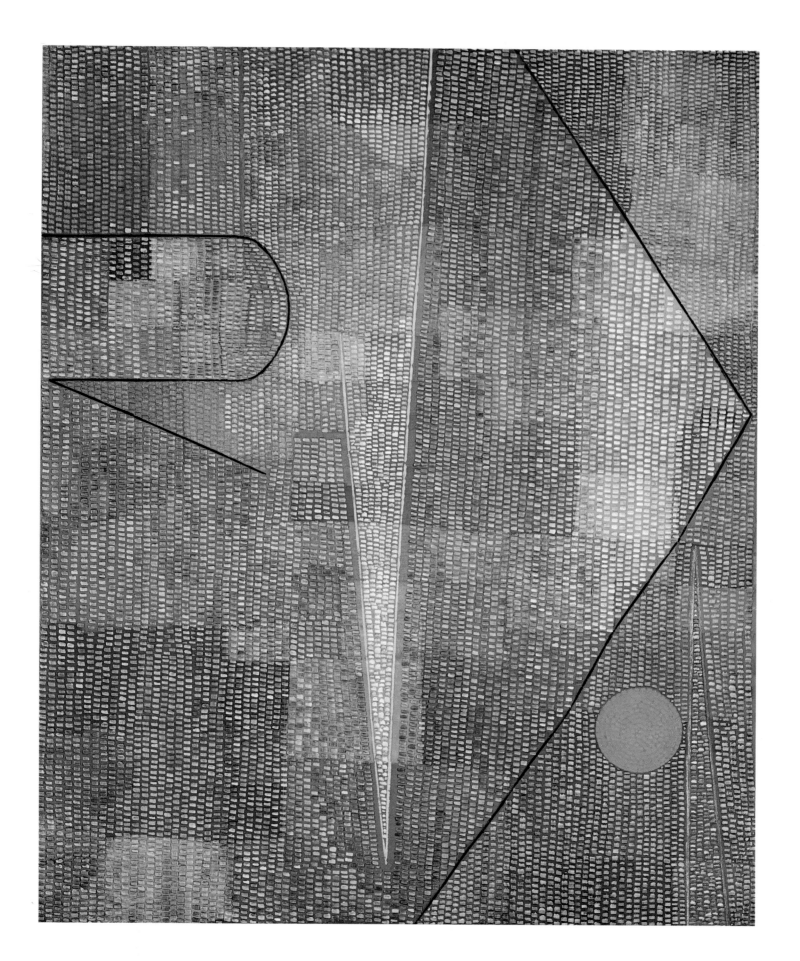

Arab Song, 1932

Endlessly experimenting with the pictorial possibilities offered by new materials, Klee painted several works on jute during this year. With extraordinary economy of means, he offers us a souvenir of the voyage in concentrated form. The Arab costume evokes Egypt as much as Tunisia. The layout is slightly reminiscent of certain 'cut-ups' by Picasso.

A figure doubly hidden behind its veil and behind a drape, emphasized on the right by two rows of Xs, looks out furtively towards the exterior of the canvas. Klee succeeds in creating a remarkable ambiguity between the cloth and the canvas, between the clothes and the drapes of a tent or a shop-front, by letting the weave of the jute show through. Behind these layers of cloth, the hidden figure is most certainly a young girl. A flower representing her face and a leaf for her heart indicate the nature of her song. The softness of tones prolongs the sweetness of her melody like an echo.

Open, 1933

Since 1930, the last year he spent teaching at the Bauhaus, Klee had been working periodically on problems of articulation between complex geometric structures. *Open* takes up the study of flat and stereometric projections for the last time, and produces as a final version the most complex work of the whole series.

The whole painting is presented like a grand piece of architecture, austere and enigmatic: fortress or mortuary temple, there is no real indication. The articulation of the schema does not permit a logical reconstruction of structure. In an assemblage of windowless walls, the point of an arrow indicates the only opening, which consists of a transparent space framed in blue on three sides, and connected by the fourth to an ensemble of articulated, suspended designs. The opacity of all the other surfaces is achieved by means of a mixture of water-colour and wax. The introduction of a red disc increases the disquieting nature of the image. But perhaps, after all, he was only forming a rigorous construction of the static/dynamic opposition which had pre-occupied him throughout his teaching period.

Scholar, 1933

Hitler's coming to power in January 1933 intensified the war against modern art, which was considered 'degenerate'. The Dusseldorf academy was directly attacked in the newspapers. The residence that Klee still kept in Dessau was searched. In April his teaching practice was suspended, and in the autumn he was definitively dismissed. Having become a non-desirable in the Berlin galleries, he took off on a trip to Paris to sign a contract with the dealer D. H. Kahnweiler. On 23rd December, he finally decided to emigrate to Bern, the city of his birth.

In the midst of this personal upheaval, his correspondence shows him calm and serene in the face of adversity. Even with a foreboding of disaster, he coldly analysed events and their irreversibility. Nothing of his sadness, his fears or disappointment came through.

It is difficult to determine exactly when he painted *Scholar*, whose tiny format seems to accentuate its intimate, confidential character. The signature, written in a different-coloured rectangle, is carried like an identity card, and we might well consider this painting as a self-portrait. The sombre tonality of the background is a thinly veiled reference to the disastrous political situation in which Klee found himself. A simple oval rests on the drooping line of the shoulders. The point of contact between the oval and the arc of the circle seems to be suggesting that the 'head' is likely to fall off at any minute. The simple outline conveys with a single gesture all the anxiety hidden behind the knitted brows. With remarkable economy of means, Klee transmits in the same image a profound insecurity in the face of events and a determination to win through despite it all.

Figure in Garden, 1937

Jurgen Glaesemer rightly pointed out that between 1933 and 1937, Klee's potential suffered a serious decline. Under the joint pressure of exterior events and an inner insecurity, his output betrays a certain impasse in the repetition of pictorial solutions. Added to this was the illness which, during 1936, virtually put an end to any possibilities of creation or painting. His annual output, which up to then had been some two hundred works, had dropped to twenty-five for the year 1936. All the more surprising, then, was the resurgence of creativity which took place in 1937.

During the summer of this year, seventeen of his works featured in the great exhibition organized by the Third Reich, 'Degenerate Art', an exhibition whose aim was to sound the death-knell of modern art. It would be interesting to know what Klee must have thought about all this. But it seems that, from 1935 onwards, he kept silent about everything that touched him deeply. He would neither speak of his illness nor of his concern for the future.

As soon as his health permitted, Klee began work again, this time on a series of pastels on canvas which represented a fairly radical change of style in terms of the purification of pictorial means. The articulation of space now depends on the conjunction of two structuring entities: one consists of colour patterns of irregular sizes, the other of black streaks of uneven length spread like segments over different points on the surface. Abstract or figurative, these streaks organize the space in a such way that the point of vision becomes highly mobile. This serves to emphasize the ebb and flow of the perspective, the different degrees of depth. This late work shows a renewal of Klee's interest in the use of unexpected relationships, greatly enriching his means of expression. Here, for example, by using pastel on canvas rather than on paper, he is able to accentuate the possibilities of irradiation.

Harmonized Combat, 1937

Moving on from the undulating surface of *Figure in Garden*, Klee developed a series of more abstract pictures, based on the same type of articulation: *Yellow Signs, Blue Night* and *Beyond Earth*. Of all these, *Harmonized Combat* is at once the most abstract and the most 'musical'. The basic constitution is the same for the whole series: pastel on canvas pasted on to a piece of jute painted in a colour which accords with the rest of the composition and which, in a sense, frames the whole. This border produces a textural effect in the margins of the picture.

Here Klee is reworking, in a very free manner, the formal problems of rhythm that he first explored during his teaching at the Bauhaus. In fact, he is organizing a 'combat' between two rhythms. The most obvious rhythm is that of the black signs, and is the most successful in transmitting the idea of a surface in motion. The other is more subtle, depending on the use of colour designs ordered in numerical progression: three grey, four brown, five yellow, six reddish-orange. The passage from one to another is ensured by transitional planes of pink or peach. The large number of light maroon planes, sitting between all the others, thanks to their medium tonality, serve to unite the space and 'harmonize' the combat. Klee would often come back to this problem of visualization of rhythm during the following year, linking it more explicitly to dance.

Port and Sail-boats, 1937

By means of abridged forms, stripped to essentials, Klee transposes into another medium a theme he had already used in *Coast of Provence* in 1927. This is common practice in the works of 1937. He painted *Oriental Garden,* which recalls Tunisia, and *Legend of the Nile,* referring to his trip to Egypt. No longer able to go on long trips because of his health, he willingly allowed these images of past trips to resurface.

This painting is distinct from the rest of the year's output because of the absence of clearly defined colour schemes. The blurred patches around the edges and the softness of the tones produce a pastel effect. The completely arbitrary colours produce, nevertheless, a diffused light in perfect accord with the delicacy of the graphicism.

Intention, 1938

We have already noted Klee's great interest in ancient calligraphy. Jurg Spiller, who prepared a partial compilation of Klee's teachings at the Bauhaus, confirms that he was in possession of a book by Karl Weule, *Vom Kerbstock zum Alphabet. Urformen der Schrift* (From the Notch to the Alphabet. Original Forms of Writing), published in 1915. The most cursory glance through the illustrations in this book gives an insight into way Klee was able to create a personal calligraphy in the image of pictograms and ideograms of ancient civilizations. From 1938, this calligraphy was to take over almost all his work. It represents the final realization of a sentence taken from one of his courses: 'Drawing and writing are fundamentally identical.' In a letter to his son, he alludes to it directly, in terms of runes, the secret writing of the ancient Germanic languages.

Intention reveals the transformation to which the artist subjects nature during the production of a work. On the left, the more figurative signs (people, animals, plants) refer directly to nature. On the right, they have acquired an extra degree of abstraction, thanks to the intervention of the artist clearly situated 'between' nature and art. His 'intention' is precisely this construction of a work by means of signs which acquire a formal dimension with their integration into the materials. With a final layer of pink, he creates unity between the two zones, associating by colour some of the most abstract signs on the left with the surface on the right.

Always concerned with varying the bases, this time Klee uses paint mixed with gum on newspaper pasted on to jute. He thus obtains a double play between the printed characters held in reserve and those which he has invented himself. This work is part of a series of large formats done in the same year and ranks amongst the artist's major works.

Insula Dulcamara, 1938

In the title *Insula Dulcamara*, the second word brings together two Latin words, '*dulcis*' (soft, sweet) and '*amarus*' (bitter). The intrinsic contradictions in this word are without any doubt a reference to Klee's personal situation during these last years. So are the means of expression.

To the softness of the tonalities, Klee adds a discreet bitterness suggested by elements drawn from his personal inconography. In the upper half of the painting, we can identify two inverted astral signs, evoking the blind forces of destiny. The coast of this 'bitter-sweet' isle is reduced to one sinuous line, whilst out at sea a boat is passing by – a polyvalent symbol, evoking parting and travel but also fragility, as has often been the case in Klee's work since 1917. In the lower half of the picture, to the left, a serpentine line stands out. Frequently a symbol of menace, the serpent will reappear more often in the works of 1940 as will the symbol of death. We need only compare the whitish head of the central figure with phantom-like *Stern Visage* of 1939, or with *Death and Fire* of 1940, to realize that the spectre of death is looming. The other, more abstract, signs contribute to the animation of the surface. The bitter-sweet island is not a specific place; it is more a symbol for life in general, 'down here'.

Insula Dulcamara is one of the largest formats in which Klee used his hieroglyphic writing. The wide black strokes which now make up part of his repertoire lend themselves more easily to this style than the fine graphicism of his earlier works. The ensemble makes for a previously unequalled power of expression.

Outburst of fear III, 1939

Confronted with such an expression of anguish, it is difficult not to take into account the illness which was taking its toll on Klee's life. But it should not be considered as the origin of his whole output of this period, especially if one examines the totality of the 1939 drawings. It is in 1940 that his tone changes radically. Certainly Klee recognized in one of these drawings an association of forms which expressed his anguish better, because he reworked this form in water-colour. But it should not be forgotten that he often used humour to distance the events which touched him most deeply. The figure is expressing at least as much surprise at finding itself in detached pieces as it is emitting a sense of pain. The use of pallid colours would also suggest an interpretation of an image of fear.

On the other hand, this image appears alongside an important number of drawings of cut-up bodies, disarticulated puppets and acrobats, and fragmented landscapes. Not all of them are tortured in nature; they often even contain an element of humour. We move from the neutrality of *House in the Forest* to *Puppets' Drama*, passing through a whole range of subjects which permitted him to express various laughable situations, typical of the human condition.

The process is identical for the whole series. Klee draws closed forms, by means of which he recomposes in a playful spirit images to which he gives tragi-comic titles, inspired by the expression or situation of the character. The continuity of this process has all the hallmarks of a formal research process. Some of these drawings doubtless refer to his personal situation. They might even be part of a process of warding off fear. As in all of Klee's images, the levels of signification are multiple, and in the absence of documentation of his illness it is difficult to determine which of these works are directly related to it.

Park with Idols, 1939

An examination of the drawings of 1939 enables us to trace the origin of this rather extraordinary image. Klee is essentially preoccupied with the arrangement of closed forms and with giving them titles suggested by the image itself. Several drawings take the 'park' as subject. They are composed of fragments of landscape, reconstituted one with the other in order to produce a different image.

The coloured forms here arranged against a black background are extracted from a large number of these drawings. The yellow and brown forms resembling primitive statuettes are no doubt the origin of the title: *Park with Idols*. Klee often used this process of painting colours on a black background, giving his figures a phantom-like quality, as in *Moon of the Barbarians* and *Mephisto in Pallas*. This is all part of his search for ancestral origins and forms, and reiterates his interest in ancient writing.

Stern Visage, *1939*

Another of these mysterious creatures on a black background would seem to be an allusion to crossing the Styx with Charon, the boatman of Greek mythology; a boat-ride to the Kingdom of the Dead. We know that Klee referred directly to this subject in certain works of 1940, such as *Dark Boat-ride*. The matt effect of the colours mixed with gum on a black background intensifies the tenebrous nature of the experience.

But a closer examination of *Stern Visage* reveals a polysemic image of a fairly complex structure. There is no mistaking the form of the 'barge', but the 'sail' form is more ambiguous. At once a sail but also a 'stern visage', its outline resembles the letter P. And the angles formed at the meeting-point of a yellow semi-circle and the 'mast' of the sail suggest the letter K. Klee thus imposes his initials on the figure of Charon, transforming him, if not into a self-portrait, at least into a foreshadowing of that with which he would soon have to identify.

Elves, 1939

Klee often used elf- and gnome-like figures to put movement into space, as in, for example, *Dancing Game of the Red Gnomes* of 1924 and *Dance of the Spirit of the Air* of 1932. Whether drawn from Scandinavian mythology or from Germanic tales, these motifs are all creatures of darkness and night. Even in these late works, he is calling up all that is primitive and secret, all that behaves in mysterious ways. It is for the same reason that witches appear in some paintings.

Elves are spirits of the air, Nordic in origin. Coming from the earth and the water, they symbolize subterranean and nocturnal forces. Both charming (in their movement) and fearful (in their seriousness), they fascinate and enchant. Scandinavian mythology presents them carried away by nocturnal dances in the meadows, to which the background colours are perfectly suited. We know also that they invite humans to join in their dance, but afterwards, they carry them off to their death. In the painting there is perfect unity between myth and execution. Works like *Elves* show that Klee was right when, at the Iena conference in 1924, he called accusations of infantilism in his drawing 'nonsense'.

Still Feminine Angel, 1939

The angel had for a long time played a part in Klee's iconography. But as he approached his death, he produced a long series of angel motifs which are presented as a grand metaphor for the ultimate voyage which would carry him over to the side of the invisible. Through these images he delicately portrays the diverse transformations that the human face must undergo to become angelic. In fact, he shows us beings in the midst of transformation, resolutely fixed in the half-way world.

The unusual combination of materials that Klee favoured is here responsible for the effect of immateriality. He draws with grease-chalk on paper previously covered with blue paint with gum, allowing the background to show through. One eye is looking anxiously downwards over its wing, observing the remains of a disappearing sexuality. The other eye, looking upwards, is indicating the direction to be taken in order to complete the metamorphosis. In *Angel with Star*, *Vigilant Angel* and *Forgetful Angel*, it is impossible to deny that the generally smiling faces of this series represent the provisional triumph of wit over suffering.

La Belle Jardinière (A 'Biedermeier' Phantom), 1939

A direct reworking of a drawing from the same year, entitled *With Flowers*, this feminine figure, at once radiant and phantom-like, no doubt reminded Klee of the pompous style of the first half of the nineteenth century, which we look upon today with scornful amusement. This rather stiff figure, precious and somewhat measured in form, appears radiant in the centre of a garden space which is brightly coloured and luminous. The form of the head has already been the subject of study in several drawings. It is not dissimilar to certain heads in Picasso, who had been to visit Klee in Bern in November 1937. Furthermore, Klee had seen thirty of his works at an exhibition of French art in the Bern Kunsthalle in the spring of 1939.

Nevertheless, the integration of the figure into the coloured space is typical of Klee's own style. The blue and the red with which he draws the essential lines are also to be found, like a halo, in the background, assuring the passage of the figure from foreground to background.

Drummer, 1940

During the last year's of Klee's life, his pictorial output accelerated markedly. In 1939, he had recorded 1254 works in his catalogue. The first four months of 1940 account for 366. It is worth mentioning these figures because they are evidence of an uncommon will to dominate the situation. In a letter to his friend and biographer Will Grohmann, he shows perfect lucidity: 'It is not by chance that I am committed to the tragic death. Even the leaves know it and say: the time has come.'

One cannot ignore the presence of the theme of death in these last years, especially in the last months; death, the inevitability of which was becoming more and more evident. But it is necessary to be clear about its existential sense. What is being expressed is less a theme than an experience of death. After striving for his whole life to elucidate the functioning of the laws of nature in pictorial terms, his work is now in the grip of the final enigma, with which no compromise is possible. The stylistic unity of these last works is partly due to this certitude. The affirmation is more direct and acquires a power directly related to the great simplicity of the pictorial means.

Drummer is a prime example. The reduction of the face to an eye and the arms to drumsticks constitutes the essential abbreviation of this figure. Nevertheless, it succeeds in forcefully conveying the percussionist's gesture as he hammers his drum. The two red tonalities accentuate the effect of the black and add a dramatic note to the image. Several works from 1940 clearly show that Klee had a presentiment of death. One can well imagine the *Drummer* at the head of the ultimate cortège, the harbinger of the final announcement.

Death and fire, 1940

The pallid face of death, which made its first appearance in *Insula Dulcamara*, is here again, this time more insistent; alone amongst a few accessory signs. On the left, on a red incandescent surface, a three-pointed star symbolizes the forces of destiny soon to take their toll. To the right, we can recognize the figure of the boatman, Charon, with his oar; he is the liaison between life and death, an image often used in the last drawings, as in *Dark Boat-ride* and *Rowing Desperately*. As Klee no longer kept up his diaries, his works are the only evidence of the kind of dialogue that he had established between himself and the grim reaper. We know from his correspondence with his wife and son, dating from 1936, that death is omnipresent. His remaining energy was dedicated exclusively to his work, and, by force of circumstance, in total isolation.

The considerable number of works produced in these last four months shows that despite the ups and downs of his physical health, his intellectual capacity was un-impaired. According to Grohmann, his leisure time was given over to reading Aeschylus's *Oresteia*. No doubt he was feeling in perfect accord with the tragic climate of this work. As Maurice Blanchot expressed it, speaking of the writer in a similar situation: 'One could only write if one stays one's own master in the face of death. And if one establishes a dominant relationship with it' (*Literary Space*). It is in this sense of complete mastery of self that we should interpret this work. Klee's personal reflections, in this image, give way to a testament to the universal.

Flora of the Rocks, 1940

In the midst of a series of works dominated by the tragic, the subject of this piece is surprising. There is a sudden reversal, a reconsideration of the whole question of the organic model which had been for so long at the core of his teaching. A kind of 'artist's legacy', or a final achievement, it was the last painting he finished.

The incandescent effect of the light is astonishing, if only because of the subtle gradation of the reds: here we have half of the chromatic circle. The richness of colour and the luminosity, at once intense and diffuse, are extraordinary. In a completely open space, neither the flower pictograms, nor the orange areas vaguely suggesting rocks, can be definitively qualified as figurative or abstract. The organic unity which he used as a model in order to portray the unity of the work is thus perfectly realized. Each sign, surrounded by the untouched jute canvas, is perfectly integrated into the background. Klee achieves in this work a long sought-after equilibrium which denotes a total mastery over his pictorial means.

This Star Learns Humility, 1940

One could talk about the complex arsenal of pictorial means that Klee had at his disposal during his whole life and still miss the point. Amongst all the other catalogued works, this totally stripped image reveals, more than any other, the profundity of Klee's feelings in the face of death.

Without recourse to Greek mythology, or to his long meditation on the transformation of beings, he draws two schematic figures, bent under a heavy bar. A minimum of black, broad and definite strokes, painted directly with the brush on a bright blue background, evince his lucidity of spirit. There is no ambiguity in the title. *This Star Learns Humility* speaks directly about his condition. Glaesemer pointed out the intimate relationship between this last series of drawings and the evolution of Klee the person, a kind of last testament.

SELECTED BIBLIOGRAPHY

Klee's Writings

'Schöpferische Konfession', in 'Tribune der Kunst und Zeit.' no XIII, Berlin, Erich Reiss Verlag, 1920, p. 28–40.
'Tagebücher von Paul Klee, 1898–1918', Köln, Puliant Schauberg, 1957.
'Das bildnerische Denken', texts collected and annotated by Jürg Spiller, Basel/Stuttgart, Schwabe, 1956.
'Théorie de l'art moderne', selection of texts collected and translated by Pierre Henri Gonthier, Paris, Denoel/Gonthier, 1964.
'Unendliche Naturgeschichte', texts collected and annotated by Jürg Spiller, Basel/Stuttgart, Schwabe, 1970.
'Beiträge zur bildnerischen Formlehre', facsimile edited by Jürgen Glaesemer, Basel/Stuttgart, Schwabe, 1979.
'Briefe an die Familie – Band 1, 1893–1906'; 'Band 2, 1907–1940', edited by Felix Klee, Köln, Dumont 1979.

Works on Klee

FERRIER, Jean-Louis, 'Paul Klee, les années 20', Paris, Denoël, 1971.
GEELHAAR, Christian, 'Paul Klee et le Bauhaus', Neuchâtel, Ides et Calendes, 1972.
GLAESEMER, Jürgen, 'Paul Klee, les oeuvres en couleur du Kunstmuseum de Berne', Bern, Kornfeld, 1978.
GROHMANN, Will, 'Paul Klee', Geneva, Trois Collines, 1954.
KERSTEN, Wolfgang, 'Paul Klee, Zerstörung, der Konstruktion zuliebe?' Marburg, Jonas Verlag, 1987.
KLEE, Felix, 'Paul Klee par lui-même et par son fils Felix Klee', Paris/Geneva, Les Libraires associés, 1963.
NAUBERT-RISER, Constance, 'La Création chez Paul Klee', Paris, Klincksieck, 1978.
—— 'Klee, vie et oeuvre', Fribourg, Office du Livre (to be published).
PIERCE, James Smith, 'Paul Klee and Primitive Art', New York, Garland Publ., 1976.
VERDI, Richard, 'Klee and Nature', New York, Rizzoli, 1984.
WERCKMEISTER, Otto Karl, 'Versuche über Paul Klee', Frankfurt/Main, Syndikat, 1981.

PRINCIPAL EXHIBITION CATALOGUES

'Paul Klee, Das Werk der Jahre 1919–1933, Gemälde, Handzeichnungen, Druckgraphik', Cologne, Kunsthalle, 11th April–4th June, 1979.
'Paul Klee, Das Frühwerk, 1883–1922,' Munich, Städtische Galerie in Lenbachhaus, 12th December 1979–2nd March 1980.
'Paul Klee, œuvres de 1933 à 1940,' Nîmes, Musée des Beaux Arts, 1984.
'Klee', Martigny, Pierre Gianadda foundation, 24th May–3rd November 1985.
'Klee et la Musique,' Paris, Musée national d'art moderne, Centre Georges Pompidou, 10th October 1985–1st January 1986.
'Paul Klee', New York, Museum of Modern Art, 12th February–5th May 1987.

CHRONOLOGY

1879
Birth of Paul Klee on 18th December at Münchenbuchsee near Bern. His father, a music teacher at a teachers' training school at Berne-Hofwyl is German; his mother Swiss.

1880
The Klee family (mother, father, Paul and sister Mathilde, born in 1876) settle in Bern.

1886
Klee attends primary school and the Bern Gymnasium. Attains a 'Maturity' diploma.

1898
Klee moves to Munich to enrol in the Knirr School of art.

1899
He meets Lily Stumpf, a pianist (born in 1876), daughter of a Munich doctor. She will become his wife in 1906.

1900
Klee enrols at the Munich Academy and joins Franz Stuck's studio. He takes courses in art history, studies anatomy, practises modelling and begins work on etching.

1901
He leaves the Academy and, in the company of Hermann Haller, takes a trip to Italy.

1902
In May he returns to Bern where he stays until 1906.

1903
Klee completes his first ten etchings 'in severe style.'

1905
Klee produces his first 'sous-verres'. He goes to Paris with his Swiss friends Hans Bloesch and Louis Moilliet. He visits the Louvre and the Luxembourg Museum.

1906
Klee exhibits ten etchings at the Sezession in Munich. He takes a trip to Berlin (with Bloesch). In September, he marries Lily Stumpf. In October he settles in Munich.

1907
He sees the French impressionists in a Munich gallery. His Swiss friend Ernst Sondereger introduces him to Ensor and Daumier. The birth of his only son, Felix, on 30th November.

1909
At the Munich Sezession he sees eight paintings by Cézanne and finds him the master 'par excellence.' He plans to illustrate Voltaire's 'Candide'. The Sezession exhibits some of his work.

1910
Klee exhibits 56 of his works (1907–1910) at the Bern Museum, at the Zurich Kunsthaus and in a gallery in Winterthur. One of his drawings is acquired by Alfred Kubin.

1911
Klee starts work on his illustrations for 'Candide.' He meets Auguste Macke and Kandinsky at Louis Moilliet's house. Soon afterwards he meets Franz Marc and Alexey Jawlensky. He becomes part of a newly-formed group called 'Der Blaue Reiter.' He begins a catalogue of his work, minutely-detailed, which he kept up until his death.

1912
Klee takes part in the second exhibition of the 'Blaue Reiter' group in the Gottz gallery, showing only drawings and etchings. In April he visits Paris, meets Delaunay and La Fouconnier and goes to the galleries of Wilhelm Uhde, Kahnweiler and Bernheim Jeune.

1913
Klee exhibits in the Sturm gallery owned by H. Walden in Berlin and takes part in the first German Autumn Salon in the same gallery. The exhibition presents an enormous selection of European modern art (360 pictures).

1914
Klee is one of the founders of the New Munich Sezession, a group instigated by the critic Wilhelm Hausenstein. April: journey to Tunisia with Moilliet and Macke. Returns to Munich 25th April. 1st August: war breaks out. 16th August: Macke killed in Champagne.

1916
4th March: Franz Marc killed at Verdun.
11th March: Klee mobilized in the *Landsturm*.
He is sent first to Landshut, then to Schlessheim where he is stationed in an air-force depot.

1917
16th January: transferred to Gersthofen near Augsburg where he is employed as pay-clerk.
He exhibits at the *Sturm* gallery and sells several works.

1918
Klee stays at Gersthofen until after the armistice. Around Christmas, he is demobilized and returns to his family in Munich. In Berlin, Walden publishes the *Sturm-Bilderbuch* made up of drawings from *Der Sturm*, including fifteen drawings by Klee.

1919
Klee rents a large studio in the Suresnes Palace in Munich. The painters Willi Baumeister and Oskar Schlemmer try to have him engaged as professor at the Stuttgart Academy but he is turned down.
He signs a contract with the dealer Goltz in Munich.

1920
Klee has an extensive exhibition in Munich at Goltz's gallery with 362 works on view. The Berlin review *Tribüne der Kunst und Zeit*, edited by Kasimir Edschmid publishes *Creative Confession*, begun in 1918.
H. von Wedderkop and L. Zahn each devotes a monograph to him. In November, he is invited by Walter Gropius to become a professor at the Bauhaus, formed the year before in Weimar.

1921
Klee leaves Munich for Weimar. Wilhelm Hausenstein publishes his monograph *Kairuan* or *The History of the Painter Klee and the Art of our Time.*

1923
Klee publishes *Ways of Studying Nature* in *Staatliches Bauhaus in Weimar 1919–1923*. He spends the summer on the island of Baltrum in the North Sea. He meets Kurt Schwitters and El Lissitzky in Hanover.

1924
First Klee exhibition in the United States, in New York. Foundation in Weimar of the *Blauen Vier* group (the Four Blues): Kandinsky, Klee, Feininger, Jawlensky.
Journey to Sicily (Taormina, Mazzaro, Syracuse, Gela).
Klee gives a lecture in Iena *On Modern Art*, not published until 1945. 26th December: the Bauhaus closes down at Weimar.

1925
April: Bauhaus teachers and pupils settle in Dessau.
Klee publishes his *Pedagogical Sketches* in the *Bauhaus-Bucher* series. Second large exhibition of 214 works in the Goltz gallery. He takes part in the first exhibition of Surrealist painters at the Galerie Pierre in Paris. First one-man exhibition in Paris in the Galerie Vavin-Raspail.

1926
Klee travels in Italy (Elba, Pisa, Florence, Ravenna).
Inauguration of the new Bauhaus building, constructed by Gropius.

1927
Visits to Porquerolles and Corsica.

1928
Klee visits Brittany and Belle-Ile.
The *Kleegesellschaft* founded by the collector, Otto Ralfs of Brunswick, offers him a trip to Egypt, from 17th December 1928 to 17th January 1929. In the *Bauhaus* review he publishes *Exact Experiments in the Realm of Art*.

1929
Klee goes to the South of France (Carcassonne, Bayonne, the Gascony Gulf.) Excursion to San Sebastian and Pamplona. For his fiftieth birthday the Flechtheim Gallery in Berlin organizes a large exhibition of his works. Exhibition in the Galerie Bernheim Jeune in Paris. Will Grohmann publishes a monograph in the *Cahiers d'Art* in Paris.

1930
Klee spends some time in the Engadine and at Viareggio. Another exhibition in Flechtheim's gallery. Exhibition in the Museum of Modern Art, New York.

1931
1st April: Klee terminates his contract with the Bauhaus and accepts the chair offered him by the Düsseldorf Academy. A second trip to Sicily (Syracuse, Ragusa, Agrigento, Palermo, Monreale).

1932
Klee sees a Picasso exhibition at the Zurich Kunsthaus. Under pressure from the Nazis he leaves Dessau for Berlin.

1933
Journey to the South of France – Saint Raphael, Hyères, Port-Cros. Klee violently attacked by the Nazis and finally dismissed. He leaves Germany and settles permanently in Switzerland. Installs himself once more in Bern where his father and sister still live.

1934
In Germany, Grohmann publishes a first collection of drawings (1921–1930); the book is confiscated by the Nazis.

1935
Major retrospective at the Bern Kunsthalle.
First symptoms of the illness – scleroderma – which will lead to his death five years later.

1936

He works very little. He undergoes treatment at Tarasp and Montana; no appreciable success.

1937

Klee resumes his work. Picasso visits him in Bern. He sees Kandinsky for the last time on the occasion of an exhibition of his works at the Bern Kunsthalle.

The Nazis include seventeen works in an exhibition of 'degenerate art' – first in Munich then all around Germany.

They confiscate 102 of them from public collections and auction them.

1939

Klee visits Geneva and sees an exhibition of masterpieces from the Madrid Prado. He receives a visit from Georges Braque.

1940

Major Klee exhibition at the Zürich Kunsthaus (works from 1935 to 1940).

10th May: Klee enters the sanatorium at Orsolina near Locarno.

8th June: he is moved to the Sant' Agnese Clinic at Muralto-Locarno.

29th June: he dies of paralysis of the heart.

PHOTOGRAPH CREDITS

LIST OF ILLUSTRATIONS

mounted on cardboard, 22.6 × 23.2 cm. Museum der Stadt, Ulm.

51: *Motif from Hammaret, 1914/57*, oil on card, 27 × 22 cm. Kunstmuseum, Oeffentliche Kunstammlung, Basel.

53: *Kakendaemonisch, 1916/73*, water-colour on canvas, plaster base, mounted on cardboard, 18.5 × 25 cm. Kunstmuseum, Paul Klee Foundation, Bern.

55: *Coloured Angles, 1917/50*, water-colour on paper, 19.2 × 14 cm. Private collection, Switzerland.

57: *Ab Ovo, 1917/130*, water-colour on chalk-prepared paper, set on gauze backed with cardboard, 14.5 × 26 cm. Kunstmuseum, Paul Klee Foundation, Bern.

59: *Harbour at Night*, 1917/106, water-colour and gouache on paper and aeroplane canvas, prepared with plaster and backed with cardboard, 21 × 15.5 cm. Musée des Beaux-Arts, Strasbourg.

61: *Under a Black Star, 1918/116*, gouache on gauze prepared with plaster 20.5 × 15.5 cm. Kunstmuseum, Basel.

63: *Composition with Windows (Composition with the letter B), 1919/156*, india ink and oil on cardboard backed with cardboard, 50.4 × 30.3 cm. Kunstmuseum, Paul Klee Foundation, Bern.

65: *Perspective of an Occupied Room*, 1921/24, oil drawing (traced) and water-colour on paper backed with cardboard, 48.5 × 31.7 cm. Kunstmuseum, Paul Klee Foundation, Bern.

67: *K. N. The Smith, 1922/173*, oil on gauze glued on cardboard, 32.8 × 35.6 cm. Musée national d'art moderne, Centre Georges Pompidou, Paris. Donation Nina Kandinsky.

69: *Fragment from a Ballet for the Aeolian harp, 1922/87*, water-colour on paper, 23.5 × 20.3 cm. Galerie Rosengart, Lucerne.

71: *The Twittering Machine, 1922/151*, oil drawing (traced) and water-colour on paper backed with cardboard, 63.8 × 48.1 cm. Museum of Modern Art, New York.

73: *Senecio (Soon an Old Man), 1922/181*, oil on linen, 40.5 × 38 cm. Kunstmuseum, Basel.

75: *Eros, 1923/115*, pen drawing and water-colour on paper backed with cardboard, 24.5 × 33.3 cm. Galerie Rosengart, Lucerne.

77: *Aimiable Look, 1923/54*, oil on black paper 32 × 24 cm. Private collection, Switzerland.

79: *Child on the Steps, 1923/59*, oil on wood. 29 × 42 cm. Musée de Peinture et de Sculpture, Grenoble.

81: *Landscape with Yellow Birds, 1923/32*, water-colour and gouache on paper, 35.5 × 44 cm. Private collection, Switzerland.

83: *Carnival in the Mountains, 1914/114*, water-colour (brush-drawing) on paper prepared with coloured chalk, backed with cardboard, 26.5 × 33 cm. Kunstmuseum, Paul Klee Foundation, Bern.

85: *Ancient Sonority, 1925/236*, oil on cardboard. 38 × 38 cm. Kunstmuseum, Basel.

87: *Florentine Villas, 1926/223*, oil on cardboard, 49.5 × 36.5 cm. Musée National d'Art Moderne, Centre Georges Pompidou, Paris.

89: *Coast of Provence 6, 1927/234*, water-colour on paper. 22.8 × 30 cm. Private collection, New York.

91: *Chosen Site, 1927/238*, pen-drawing and water-colour on paper. 57.8 × 40.5 cm. Private collection, Munich.

93: *Highways and Byways, 1929/90*, oil on linen, 83.7 × 39.5 cm. Private collection, Switzerland.

95: *Before the Snow, 1929/319*, water-colour on paper backed with cardboard, 33.5 × 39.5 cm. Private collection, Switzerland.

97: *Individualized Measurement of the Strata, 1930/82*, pastel with gum on black paper backed with cardboard. 46.8 × 34.8 cm. Kunstmuseum, Paul Klee Foundation, Bern.

99: *Rythmical, 1930/203*, oil on jute. 69.6 × 50.5 cm. Musée National d'Art Moderne, Centre Georges Pompidou, Paris.

101: *Gleiten (Slipping/Floating), 1930/N*, oil on silk, 34 × 43 cm. Private collection.

103: *Ad Parnassum, 1932/274*, oil on canvas, 100 × 126 cm. Kunstmuseum, Paul Klee Foundation, Bern.

105: *Arab Song, 1932/283*, gouache on sacking, 91 × 64 cm. The Phillips Collection, Washington.

107: *Open, 1933/306*, water-colour and wax, muslin on wood, 40.5 × 55 cm. Private collection, Switzerland.

109: *Scholar, 1933/286*, gouache on gauze prepared with plaster, 35 × 26.5 cm. Private collection, Switzerland.

111: *Figure in Garden, 1937/129*, pastel on linen, 50 × 42.5 cm. Private collection, Switzerland.

113: *Harmonized Combat, 1937/206*, pastel on linen, 57 × 86 cm. Kunstmuseum, Paul Klee Foundation, Bern.

115: *Port and Sail-boats, 1937/151*, oil on canvas, 80 × 60.5 cm. Musée National d'Art Moderne, Centre Georges Pompidou, Paris.

117: *Intention, 1938/126*, paint mixed with glue on newspaper re-mounted on sacking. 75 × 112 cm. Kunstmuseum, Paul Klee Foundation, Bern.

119: *Insula Dulcamara, 1938/481*, oil and paint mixed with gum on newspaper re-mounted on sacking, 88 × 176 cm. Kunstmuseum, Paul Klee Foundation, Bern.

121: *Outburst of Fear III, 1939/124*, water-colour on paper, prepared with egg, backed with cardboard, 63.5 × 48.1 cm. Private collection, Switzerland.

123: *Park with Idols, 1939/282*, water-colour on black paper, 32.7 × 20.9 cm. Private collection, Switzerland.

125: *Stern Visage, 1939/857*, water-colour and tempera on newspaper prepared with gum and backed with cardboard, 33 × 21 cm. Kunstmuseum, Paul Klee Foundation, Bern.

127: *Elves, 1939/1004*, water-colour on canvas, 23.5 × 34 cm. Private collection, Switzerland.

129: *Still Feminine Angel, 1939/1016*, coloured crayons on paper prepared with blue paint mixed with gum, backed with cardboard, 41.7 × 29.4 cm. Kunstmuseum, Paul Klee Foundation, Bern.

131: *La Belle Jardinière (A 'Biedermeier' Phantom), 1939/1237* (title originally in French). Tempera and oil on sack stretched over the frame, 95 × 70 cm. Kunstmuseum, Paul Klee Foundation, Bern.

133: *Drummer, 1940/270*, paint mixed with gum on paper backed with cardboard, 34.5 × 22 cm. Kunstmuseum, Paul Klee Foundation, Bern.

135: *Death and Fire, 1940/132*, oil and paint mixed with gum on sack stretched over the frame, 46 × 44 cm. Kunstmuseum, Paul Klee Foundation, Bern.

137: *Flora of the Rocks, 1940/343*, oil and tempera on sack stretched over the frame, 90 × 70 cm. Kunstmuseum, Paul Klee Foundation, Bern.

139: *This Star Learns Humility, 1940/344*, colours mixed with gum on paper, 37.5 × 41.5 cm. Private collection, Switzerland.